POWER EVANGELISM

Signs and Wonders Today

John Wimber

with Kevin Springer

HODDER AND STOUGHTON
LONDON SYDNEY AUCKLAND TORONTO

Dedicated to my wife Carol
without whom none of these things
would have meaning.

British Library Cataloguing in Publication Data
Wimber, John
    Power evangelism: signs and wonders today.
    1. Evangelistic work   2. Miracles
    I. Title
    253.7   BV3790

    ISBN 0 340 38299 6

Copyright © 1985 by John Wimber and Kevin Springer
First printed 1985

CONTENTS

FOREWORD

My late husband, David Watson, would have been thrilled to have seen this book in print. I remember him urging John Wimber to write such a book when we visited his home in 1983.

I first heard of the existence of the author when David returned from one of his yearly visits to Fuller Theological Seminary in Pasadena, California in 1980. David and his Team conducted seminars about Church Renewal and Evangelism for the Doctor of Ministry and Master of Divinity courses. He always found his time at Fuller stimulating but I could see on his return that particular year that something new had happened and it was obviously very important. He was so excited as he proceeded to tell me of an amazing church he had visited and its pastor, John Wimber. David had only agreed to visit the church after some persuasion as his schedule at Fuller was always packed and there was little time for anything else. I was apprehensive when he started to tell me about this new friend he had made. I wasn't sure where all this would lead. I was jealous too. David could see his news was getting a rather cool reception!

Later, John and his wife Carol, together with a Team visited us in York and I could see God at work in dramatic ways. I felt totally out of my depth which surprised me as I thought I had quite a large capacity for entering into the new things the Spirit was doing. At one point I remember sitting in the pew at the beginning of a service and praying 'O Lord, I don't know if I like all this. It's so untidy and rather frightening and it might disrupt all that is going on at St. Michael's'. The Lord answered 'Well, Anne, I like it. I am in charge of St. Michael's and I will work in the way I want to.' I asked for forgiveness and help for my

constricted attitudes. I realised how close I had come to quen-
ching the Holy Spirit.

Even when David and I visited the Vineyard Church and spent
ten hilarious days with John and Carol I struggled with the Spirit.
He seemed to be doing extraordinary things and wanting me to
join in! I was quite happy to let other people lay hands on the sick
and see them healed but when it came to my participation I
wished I was a thousand miles away. To complicate matters
further David was enjoying every minute of it and ministering
with great joy. My faith to really believe in the power of God in
areas that I had no experience in was being put to the test, but as
John writes in this book 'miracles occur when we know our own
inadequacy'.

Negative reactions often precede the movement of God's
Spirit in new ways. Moses did not want to go and confront
Pharaoh but subsequent events demonstrated the power of God
dramatically; Gideon was very sceptical and fearful when God
called him and it took two miracles to persuade him to agree;
even the Virgin Mary had questions when the Angel Gabriel
brought God's news that she would conceive a son miraculously.
The disciples were clearly anxious when it came to feeding 5000
people with two loaves and five small fish! The Pharisees, when
faced with the power of God in a new way in the life and ministry
of Jesus, let tradition and self-interest become weapons against
the Spirit. God is not averse to human reactions but in the end we
need to acknowledge his sovereignty.

It is my hope that this book will help many of God's people to
see in the miraculous ministry of Jesus just how God has planned
to bring life to the world. The Holy Spirit is as eager today to
demonstrate the power of God's love as he was then. Let us work
through our fears and reactions until we can say 'here I am,
Lord, use me'.

ANNE WATSON

ACKNOWLEDGMENTS

There are many people whose support through prayer and suggestions aided the writing of this book. First, I would like to thank my mentor, partner, and friend, C. Peter Wagner, who introduced me not only to church growth but also to the church around the world. Without his encouragement and insights, I could not have written this book. I am also thankful for the late George Ladd, whose pioneering work on the kingdom of God forms the theological foundation for power evangelism.

The faculty of the School of World Missions at Fuller Theological Seminary sponsored and encouraged MC:510 – The Miraculous and Church Growth, a course in which much of the material in this book was developed.

A special thanks to Suzanne Springer, my co-author's wife, and Kevin Perrotta, managing editor of Pastoral Renewal, who put many hours into reading, commenting, and editing the early drafts. Their corrections and suggestions improved the book immensely.

Most of all I thank Jesus for so graciously working in my life, showing me more of his kingdom and compassion, despite my many shortcomings and failures. To him be all glory, blessing, and praise.

All biblical quotes are taken from the New International Version (NIV), unless otherwise indicated.

ABOUT THIS BOOK

Since 1981 I, along with C. Peter Wagner, who is professor of record, have been teaching a course at Fuller Theological Seminary, Pasadena, California, called 'MC:510 – The Miraculous and Church Growth'. Most of this book is based on material and experiences in the course, as well as my experiences as pastor of the Vineyard Christian Fellowship in Anaheim, California.

You will notice that I describe the basis for *Power Evangelism* as both scriptural and personal experience of the miraculous. Scripture must always be the primary source and basis for our practice. But our experience of scriptural truth makes it come alive, pressing it deeply into our hearts.

The experiences described in these pages occurred in the classrooms at Fuller Seminary, during Sunday gatherings, at conferences in the United Kingdom and across the United States, in the streets and on aeroplanes. So while the book's core is scriptural instruction about signs and wonders, personal testimony (mine and others) will help demonstrate and illustrate what is taught.

My hope and goal is to provide a new perspective on old information – a new understanding of biblical accounts of the supernatural, and how they apply to us today. Most of the biblical passages quoted will no doubt be familiar to the reader. It is their application that will be new.

Related to this is a difficulty that my co-author, Kevin Springer, and I encountered: in a book we cannot lead you through practical workshops in which you experience what we describe. This is a major concern because, as you shall see, it is the actual *doing* of the works of Christ – including signs and wonders – that is intended to be a part of the normal Christian life.

I do not believe that it is enough for Christians to gather information, understand new facts – even think differently about the supernatural in scripture – if it does not affect how we live. The purpose of all our learning is to experience and advance the kingdom of God, and this is a second goal of the book. Stated differently, we want to help you learn new skills and apply them to how you live your Christian life, especially in the practice of personal evangelism.

Though this is more difficult to accomplish in a book, we provide numerous illustrations and ample practical instruction to take personal action concerning what is taught.

When the disciples approached Jesus regarding their failure – and his success – at driving out a demon who for years had been tormenting a boy, he provided a simple response. 'You have so little faith', he said, '. . . if you have faith as small as a mustard seed, you can say to this mountain, "Move from here to there" and it will move. Nothing will be impossible for you' (Matthew 17:20–21).

Faith. The very smallest amount of it. That is probably the most important prerequisite for experiencing God's power today. It is my hope that this book will help add that tiny speck of belief, so God can move large mountains through you.

JOHN WIMBER
Yorba Linda, California
June, 1985

1

THE KINGDOM OF GOD

It all started in 1962.

A new Christian, I was to attend my first church service. I was excited about what God would do in the gathering. I was also naive; I had rarely attended church services as a non-Christian.

Having created an idealised picture of church life, built from only a few weeks of gleaning scripture, I was unprepared for what awaited. I anticipated training in spiritual warfare and equipping to advance the kingdom of God. I envisioned Christians coming together, singing and praying, receiving encouragement or exhortation from scripture, then dispersing throughout Orange county, California, to perform dramatic healings, expel demonic spirits, oppose evil authorities. Then, I thought, we would return later in the day with new converts and reports of great miracles, overflowing with joy and worshipping God. It was a vision taken from the book of Acts.

What I soon discovered was that most Christians do not come together to prepare for battle with Satan and conquer territory for Jesus Christ. They enjoyed talking *about* the battle. They usually prayed for victory. They sang and preached about the need to advance God's kingdom, even weeping for it. And then they went home to live secure lives, far from the battlefields. Christian doctrine, so tenaciously defended, was circumscribed by business, family, and recreational commitments. Upon reflection now, after my first church service I felt cheated, because I had joined Christ's army in order to do his works.

When I became a Christian only a week earlier, I recalled a long-forgotten incident. I remembered seeing a man who used to roam the streets of downtown Los Angeles wearing sandwich boards. The front said 'I'm a fool for Christ' and the back said 'Who's fool are you?' I remembered mocking that man – just another religious lunatic walking the streets, I thought at the time. A strange recollection. Nevertheless Christ spoke powerfully to me through it. He told me that I, too, must be willing to be a fool for him. Whatever he asked me to do – regardless of the financial, emotional, or physical cost – I was to obey.

That was how I began an uneasy relationship with the church, a relationship that has always been both a blessing and challenge. A blessing because the church is where Jesus rules; a challenge because so few Christians – including myself for many years – understand the gospel of the kingdom of God.

Perhaps it was the shock and disappointment of that first church service, but I was never fully satisfied with typical evangelical church life. (Do not misunderstand me: I am a committed evangelical Christian, grateful for the rich heritage that I have benefited from over the years.)

Probably the more fundamental reason for my restlessness regarding the church is my background. I grew up in Anaheim, California, after moving there from the midwest, and lived in the area that is now Disneyland. I was raised a pagan – a fourth generation unbeliever – having never belonged to a church before the age of 29. I was not integrated into Christian culture – and it was not integrated into me. I was a man of the world.

By the time I reached my early teens my entire focus was on music. I entered the music business at that time, starting with local Orange county bands and eventually moving on to involvement with bands with national exposure and a few that even gained international attention. By 1962, my career was soaring. I worked with several bands, such as a Las Vegas show group and a rock-and-roll group called the Righteous Brothers.

But my personal life was in shambles. My wife, Carol, and I had been married for seven years and had three children. My lifestyle was not conducive to a stable marriage. Soon after the birth of our third child, Carol separated from me. It looked like a divorce was impending.

In the midst of the heartbreak of separation, I began seeking God in my own way. One morning I went out in the desert to watch the sun rise, hoping for a religious experience. I began reflecting on my life, growing more and more despondent. Soon I was weeping. Then I screamed, 'Oh God, if you're there, help me'.

Returning to my hotel, embarrassed and confused ('Get a hold of yourself', I kept thinking), I was greeted by a message that my wife wanted to talk with me. I phoned Carol and she asked that I come and get her; she wanted to give our marriage one more chance. Naturally I thought this was answered prayer.

Eventually we moved back to California. We continued to have marriage problems. But I did not stop talking with God. Soon I was to attend a church service. Carol had been raised a Catholic and thought that we should be remarried in the Catholic Church. So one of my few pre-Christian church experiences was my remarriage ceremony. (At that time we promised never again to use the word divorce. We haven't.)

A second experience of a church service came on the heels of my remarriage ceremony, after I had begun a more serious search for God, but still was an unbeliever. For me, this service was incomprehensible, particularly because I was a professional jazz musician – a pre-hippie hippie – who knew nothing about Christianity or any organised religion. The preacher used language full of jargon, technical terms, and affected diction (to me he made no sense at all); the music, sincerely sung, was dreadful; the people related to me strangely – uneasy about my smoking, hostile to my swearing. I was intruding in their lives. They were not comfortable with me there, nor was I. It was not a pleasant encounter.

Despite this experience, a short time later Carol and I became committed Christians through a home Bible study group. The patience, warmth, and sincerity of the Bible-study leader, combined with my hunger for God, broke me open like a ripe watermelon to God's grace.

And, again despite the shortcomings of the church, I returned for many more services, eventually becoming a member. Over the next seven years I led hundreds of people to faith in Christ, becoming the assistant pastor in 1970 and later the co-pastor. By then we had a new building to accommodate all the people who had been brought into the congregation.

Even as a successful pastor, I remained uneasy, always sensing the gap between the early disciples' experience as they spread the gospel of the kingdom of God, and what my congregation experienced.

Eventually I left the pastorate (a story I will tell in greater detail later), but my uneasy relationship with the church continued. I still felt cheated when I attended church, as though I had committed my life to something that was being withheld from me.

Then I began to learn about the kingdom of God, and the church – indeed, my Christian life – took on an entirely new meaning. I no longer dread Sunday mornings. They are what in my youthful naivete I had envisioned they should be: exciting gatherings in which the people of God are equipped to go out and preach and demonstrate the gospel.

This book tells of the key elements in my growth that led to changes in a church that I now pastor, the Vineyard Christian Fellowship in Anaheim, California. While signs and wonders are what many visitors first notice about our church life, my understanding and experience of them come from an investigation of the kingdom of God – not out of a thirst for the supernatural. In this chapter I will present the biblical and theological key to experiencing signs and wonders today, the basis and motivation for joining the fight against Satan.[1]

A political kingdom

The good news Jesus preached was the gospel of the kingdom of God. 'The time has come,' Christ preached, 'The kingdom of God is near. Repent and believe the good news!' (Mark 1:15). What did the term 'kingdom of God' mean to Christ and his listeners? Where did it come from? Through the parables – and their interpretations which were usually given privately to the disciples – Christ transformed what was commonly accepted about the kingdom of God in his day. To understand what was assumed by first-century Jews, we must begin by looking at the kingdom of God in the Old Testament.

For most of their history the Jews lived under the domination of evil nations. Decline began after King David, with Israel dividing between north and south at Solomon's death. The Jews began to think of a time in the future when God would restore the Davidic blessings of the past.

At this time the concept of the Day of the Lord arose. The prophets coined this phrase, in which people understood that

God was going to establish a military kingdom. They sought salvation in a nationalistic and geographic realm free from foreign kings. They were looking for an empire like the 'good old days' of King David.[2] But it was a two-sided coin, and the flip-side of salvation was judgement, the judgement of the nations and even of Israel (see Amos 1).

After the dispersion of the ten northern tribes and the Babylonian captivity of the southern tribes, hope in the fulfilment of the Day of the Lord appeared (Psalm 126). Under Zerubbabel, a descendant of David, people thought the kingdom would be established. But with Zerubbabel's disappearance, their aspirations were dashed. Still, they never stopped looking for the Anointed One – the Messiah – to lead them to political power through military might.

This appears to be what the Jews in general were looking for at the time of Christ, and it is in these terms they understood him when he spoke of the kingdom. The sixth chapter of John clearly supports this. The people wanted Jesus to become King (verse 15). Even the disciples, after being with him for years, longed for this (Acts 1:6).

In summary, the prophets presented the kingdom of God – what they called the Day of the Lord – as a kingdom of this world, peopled by Jews. It was not a spiritual and other-worldly kingdom: it was the dream of Jewish nationalism.[3]

Caught between two ages

But this was not the only popularly accepted understanding of the kingdom of God in Christ's days. During the intertestamental period (approximately 400 BC to the New Testament era), the time in which the Apocryphal literature[4] was written, the term 'kingdom of God' came into widespread usage. As was true for the Day of the Lord, hope was prominent, but it assumed a new meaning. The hope of the prophets was for a historical, political kingdom. The Apocryphal writers saw an end coming to the present age, with God creating a new world in which all evil, demons, sickness, and death would be defeated.[5]

This 'present age' was thought to be dominated by Satan. The idea came out of the frightful persecutions unleashed by Antiochus Epiphanes, the king of Syria from 175 to 164 BC who tried

to hellenise the Jews, inciting the revolt of the Maccabees. The
Jews believed that such hell on earth was the result of cosmic
turmoil.

In the Pseudepigraphic Book of Jubilees, the 23rd chapter, the
age to come (the Golden Age) is ushered in by God himself.[6] It
reverses the evils of Satan, who appears as the ruler of a
counter-kingdom of evil. Good triumphs. Healing and the expulsion of demons abound.

The kingdom in the New Testament

Jesus too held these views. He used the Old Testament and
intertestamental terms like the 'kingdom of God' and 'ages',
building on their popularly accepted meaning to explain why he
had come. For example, in Matthew chapter 13, verses 36 to 43,
in explaining the parable of the wheat and the weeds, he used
terms like 'sons of the kingdom', 'sons of the evil one', 'the end
of the age', and 'the righteous will shine like the sun in the
kingdom of their Father'.[7] He taught the disciples that like the
Old Testament prophets, he too saw an imminent day of judgement soon coming for the nations, the Son of Man being the
Judge. And as during the intertestamental period, he too fore-
saw a swift end coming to the present age, with a future age – 'the
kingdom of the Father' – replacing it.

George Ladd summarises scriptural teaching on the ages with
these words:

> In brief, this age, which extends from creation to the Day of
> the Lord . . . is the age of human existence in weakness and
> mortality, of evil, sin, and death. The Age to Come will see
> the realization of all that the reign of God means, and will be
> the age of resurrection into eternal life in the Kingdom of
> God. Everything in the Gospels points to the idea that life in
> the Kingdom of God in the Age to Come will be life on the
> earth – but life transformed by the kingly rule of God when
> his people enter into the full measure of the divine blessings
> (Mt. 19:28).[8]

It was with this understanding that John the Baptist made his
announcement: 'Repent, for the kingdom of heaven is near'
(Matthew 3:2). God was ready to bring the new age into exist-

ence. John announced the new age would soon be here. Jesus said, 'The kingdom of God has come upon you' (Matthew 12:28).

In the New Testament, the Greek word *basileia* means kingship or royal rule. It is normally translated 'kingdom'. It implies exercise of kingly rule or reign rather than simply a geographic realm over which a king rules. Westerners conceive of kingdoms largely in terms of realms. For example, the United Kingdom conjures thoughts of the territory encompassing British lands. The biblical concept includes being a realm too, and more. It also includes rule.

This is what Jesus meant when he said that the kingdom or rulership of God had come *in him*. The authority of God had come to claim what was rightfully his. The future age – the kingdom of God – invaded the present age – the kingdom of Satan.[9] To use an expression of George Ladd, we live in 'the presence of the future'. We are between the times, as it were, between the inauguration and the consummation of the kingdom of God.

This explains Christ's pattern of ministry, repeated wherever he went:

1 *Proclamation*: He preached repentance and the good news of the kingdom of God.

2 *Demonstration*: He cast out demons, healed the sick, raised the dead – which proved he was the presence of the kingdom, the Anointed One.

Jesus came as a Jew to Israel. He accepted the authority of the Old Testament, basically ministering to the 'lost sheep of Israel' (Matthew 10:5–7). Kingdom rule was first offered to the Jews. But Israel rejected Christ and his kingdom. Jesus was disappointed (Matthew 23:37–39). While Israel *as a nation* rejected Christ, a remnant did accept him, and these few were the foundation of the New Testament church (Romans 11:1–24). Jesus called twelve disciples, symbolising the continuity between the disciples and the twelve tribes of Israel (Matthew 19:28). By choosing the Twelve Jesus taught that he was raising up a new people to replace the nation that was rejecting his message.

Christ's blessing of Peter in the sixteenth chapter of Matthew, where Peter is given the 'keys of the kingdom of heaven', is best understood in terms of the Old Testament idea of Israel as the people of God.[10]

His announcement to Peter, 'You are Peter, and on this rock I will build my church', was in perfect continuity with Old Testament Israel's concept of building a nation. Jesus was using Old Testament images, taken from the prophets (Jeremiah 1:10; Amos 9:11–12). In the New Testament, Israel is the *church of Christ*.[11]

When Israel rejected the kingdom of God, Christ handed his rule, the place of redemption and focus of his works, over to the church (Matthew 21:33–46). Therefore, the church has the 'keys' – the way – to the kingdom. Jesus took the keys away from the Pharisees, because they had taken away the key of knowledge of the kingdom from the people (Luke 11:45–52). As George Ladd would say, the keys are the spiritual insights and authority that enabled Peter to lead others through the door of revelation. The keys are the narrow path to the kingdom of God.[12]

The authority to bind or loose involves admission or exclusion of men and women from the kingdom of God.[13] The proclamation and demonstration of the kingdom of Christ provide the opportunity for people to enter eternal life (Matthew 10:14,15,40).

Kingdoms embody three elements: a king, authority, and subjects. If one of these is missing, we do not have a kingdom. Jesus is our King; all authority in heaven and earth has been given to him by his Father; Christians are his subjects.

Some Christians, unclear about the relationship between the kingdom of God and the church, confuse the two, teaching that the church is the kingdom. This leads to serious error, such as equating church membership with final salvation. The church is an avenue to salvation, in so far as she leads people to union with Christ, but the church is not the source of salvation.

The kingdom of God brought forth the church at Pentecost through the outpouring of the Holy Spirit. The church is the primary (though not exclusive) residence of God's rule. This means the church witnesses to the kingdom but does not have authority in herself to build the kingdom; only God has that authority. When church is confused with kingdom, leaders assume that God's authority resides in their office, that they are the rule of God. Authoritarianism – even cultishness – can be an unfortunate result of this kind of thinking. When pastoral leaders understand that their authority is derived from the kingdom of God, and that rule is not equated with office, they are restrained from leading in their own authority.

The church is also the instrument of the kingdom. The disciples not only proclaimed the kingdom, they demonstrated the works and miracles of the kingdom. Jesus told Peter that the 'gates of Hades will not overcome [the church]' (Matthew 16:18). The 'gates of Hades' are the strongholds of evil and death, satanic powers that seek to destroy us (Ephesians 6:10–12).[14] As Christ's instruments, we war on these strongholds, replacing their dominion with the kingdom of God.

With this in mind Christ commissioned the twelve (Matthew 10:5–15); the seventy (Luke 10:1–20); and now us (Matthew 28:18–20). During the forty days between his resurrection and ascension, Jesus spoke to the apostles about the kingdom of God (Acts 1:3). In Samaria, Philip 'preached the good news of the kingdom of God' (Acts 8:12), and Peter, James, and Paul all mentioned the kingdom of God in their letters.

The gospel of the kingdom

Proclamation of a faulty gospel will produce faulty or at best, weak Christians. Such is the case all too often today. Instead of a call to the lordship of Christ and membership in his army, people are hearing a selfist gospel: come to Jesus and get this or that need met, be personally fulfilled, reach your potential. This is not the costly kingdom gospel that Christ proclaimed: 'Whoever wants to save his life will lose it, but whoever loses his life for me and for the gospel will save it' (Mark 8:35).

Entering the kingdom is like enlisting in the navy. But often the kingdom is likened to a Caribbean cruise on a luxury liner. Who would turn that offer down? So people change into their leisure clothes, grab their suntan lotion, and saunter down to the docks. What a shock it is when they see a large grey ship with numbers painted on the side! Even more shocking is learning that the ship is loaded with guns, cannons, jets, and helicopters. It is a warship, not a luxury cruise liner!

The same is true of the kingdom in this age: it is a warship, navigating in enemy territory.

Battle fronts

The enemy follows no rules of war. Nothing for him is unfair. Satan is not a gentleman. The sooner Christians understand this, the more serious they will become about being equipped and properly trained for kingdom warfare.

Although he follows no rules, we know Satan attacks on three fronts – the flesh, the world, and direct assaults from himself. Because this book is primarily concerned with the assaults of Satan, I will only make a few comments on the first two, devoting the remainder of the chapter to the latter.[15]

The flesh:
In the 1936 Spanish Civil War, Franco's Loyalist Army defeated the Republican Army in Madrid. It was the key battle of the war and led to the establishment of Franco's government in Spain. When asked what the key to his victory was, Franco replied, 'The Fifth Column'. He had four columns of troops, and a 'Fifth Column' of loyalists *inside* Madrid who, through sabotage, seriously weakened the Republican Army.

We too have a Fifth Column, 'sinful passions' that reside within us. In Paul's words, 'I know that nothing good lives in me, that is, in my sinful nature' (Romans 7:18). The enemy loves to exploit our Fifth Column through temptation, but God has given us the power to walk by faith and resist those temptations.

The world:
Psalm 137 says, 'How can we sing the songs of the Lord while in a foreign land?' How can Christians serve God's kingdom while taking on the values and lifestyles of the world? They cannot.

When we think of ourselves as an army, the issue of discipline and fulfilment of kingdom standards becomes more critical. Sometimes an invading army looks at civilians and says, 'Their lifestyle looks attractive. I like the glitter of materialism; the thrill of personal power; the pleasure of sexual immorality; the quest for self-fulfilment. Maybe it isn't too bad out there'. When that happens, discipline is lost, we are infiltrated, and eventually taken captive. Paul has strong advice about this: 'No one serving as a soldier gets involved in civilian affairs – he wants to please his commanding officer' (2 Timothy 2:4).

We have been given the keys to the kingdom, the authority and power over the enemy, but if we do not exercise that power, it is of no use. The kingdom of darkness is organised to distract us, to prevent us from doing God's bidding. Through the glitter of materialism and power, sexual immorality and seeking after self-fulfilment, Satan diverts our attention from the kingdom of God.

Satan's goal, then, is to get us to burn our draft cards and go absent without leave.

Fellowship with other Christians in local churches – outposts of the kingdom – is a primary defence against being taken in by the world. Prayer, scripture study, and spiritual disciplines like fasting are necessary not only to gain God's power and insight but also for equipping us to overcome the world.

The Devil:

In John 10 we read that Satan has well-defined objectives: 'The thief comes only to steal and kill, and destroy' (verse 10). We also observe in the sixth chapter of Ephesians that it is against the Devil and his demons, not men and women, whom we war.

Our situation is similar to an underground army living in a land still occupied by a defeated enemy. Such was the French underground's role after D-Day during World War II. The Germans were still capable of committing atrocities on French civilians even though the Germans' eventual defeat was sure. The 1984 arrest and forthcoming trial of Claus Barbie illustrates how barbarous their acts were: knowing there was no hope of German victory, Barbie nevertheless tortured and murdered hundreds of Frenchmen – including children. He was nicknamed 'the Butcher of Lyon'.

Satan has many names too: Destroyer, Deceiver, Liar – the Butcher of the World. In our war with Satan, there are no demilitarised zones. There is never a lull in the fighting. We are born into the fight, and – unless the Day of the Lord comes – we will die in the fight. All we should know in this world is war.

The kingdom of Satan was and is Christ's real enemy. There is a war! Jesus is about his Father's business, which is releasing those held captive by Satan. The final outcome of the battle has been assured through Christ's death, resurrection, and ascension to the place of all authority, the right hand of the Father (1 Corinthians 15:20–28).

But Satan is not yet cast out and will not be until Christ returns to establish his kingdom forever. So we are caught between two ages. The fight continues.

We are God's army, like it or not.

A draft call

In order to enter the warfare, we must correctly understand power and authority in the kingdom. In Luke 9:1–2 we read: 'When Jesus had called the Twelve together, *he gave them power and authority* to drive out all demons and to cure diseases, and he sent them out to preach the kingdom of God and to heal the sick'. He gave them power and authority to cure diseases and drive out *all* demons. Everyone, according to Acts 1:8, can receive power from the Holy Spirit. Power is the ability, the strength, the might to complete a given task. Authority is the right to use the power of God.

For example, a traffic policeman does not have the power to stop cars. However, he does stop them, because he wears a badge and uniform given him by a higher authority. We have been given a badge and uniform by Jesus. These gifts become effective when we learn to wear and use them correctly.

In scripture, the centurion understood the principle of how authority and power work (see Matthew 8:5–13). He was a man both under authority and over others. He knew how to receive and give orders. After asking Jesus to heal his paralysed servant – to which Jesus responded he would 'go and heal him' – the centurion replied: 'Just say the word, and my servant will be healed'. Jesus, 'astonished' by the centurion's words, said, 'I have not found anyone in Israel with such great faith'.

Our difficulty is that we have not learned to receive or give orders. To a great extent, we practise a cosmetic Christianity, because we have misunderstood our initial call to Christ. We think that the key for maturity and power is to be 'good'. We then focus on our behaviour but our behaviour never meets the high standards of Christ's righteousness.

I did this for years. By focusing on my behaviour, I was in constant turmoil, because my behaviour was never good enough, never meeting God's standards (or my standards) of righteousness. I first believed in Christ because I was not good, yet after becoming a Christian I still struggled in my own strength with not being good enough. So I was always under conviction, always struggling with guilt.

Then one day, sixteen years ago, after hearing a man with a similar testimony, I fell to my knees and asked God to help me. He responded, 'Since you can do nothing without me, how much help do you want'? Then he said, 'The issue is not being good, it is being God's. Just come to me, and I'll provide goodness for you'.

I did not fully understand his words. What did he mean, 'I'll provide goodness for you'? I was confused, so for the next five years I tried to be good in my own strength. I soon became more and more despondent. Finally, I began to ask God about what he had told me earlier concerning his goodness. He explained that he had good works prepared for me, but they were *his* works, and I could not do them for him. He told me that I needed to begin to listen to his voice rather than try to distil the Christian life down to a set of rules and principles. I began to listen more during my prayer and scripture study times, and more consciously talked with him throughout the normal activities of the day.

Then something interesting began to happen. He put new desires and attitudes in me. His Spirit began to strengthen me to do things I previously had no desire for. I began to hear his voice throughout the day. And good works were multiplied in my life.

Today I no longer focus on trying to be good, instead I am primarily concerned with doing God's bidding: what he commands, I do. Now my personal life is more conformed to his righteousness and character than it used to be. Following his commands does not leave much time for sin.

Most of us are confused about how to live a life of faith. We cannot understand or relate to the super-human efforts it took to do the things that Jesus did. The reason is that too often we are searching for methods, formulas, and principles that will open the power of God to us, becoming frustrated each time we learn another 'key' that does not work.

As noted above, we are not the kingdom, we are instruments of the kingdom. The works of the kingdom are performed through us, thus our purpose is to witness about what God has done, is doing, and will do. Like Jesus, we have come to do the will of the Father. When asked how we should pray, Jesus taught us, 'Our Father in heaven . . . your kingdom come, your will be done on earth as it is in heaven . . .' As the centurion did, we must learn how to hear and believe Jesus's commands if we expect to do signs and miracles.

Cosmic warfare

James Kallas, in *The Real Satan*, says:

> A war is going on! Cosmic war! Jesus is the divine invader sent by God to shatter the strengths of Satan. In that light, the whole ministry of Jesus unrolls. Jesus has one purpose – to defeat Satan. He takes seriously the strength of the enemy.[16]

Kallas's remarks raise a significant question: Does Satan attack the kingdom of God, or is Christ the 'divine invader'? And, what difference does the answer to this question mean to Christians? The difference affects our attitude and stance towards the Christian life. If Jesus is the invader, Satan is consigned to the defensive. We become offensive soldiers, taking territory, redeeming lives – Christ's cobelligerents.

Jesus says the same thing in Matthew, chapter 11: 'From the days of John the Baptist until now, the kingdom of heaven has been forcefully advancing, and forceful men lay hold of it' (verse 12). George Ladd points out that this verse may be interpreted several ways, depending on how the Greek term 'forcefully advancing' is translated. It may be understood as 'to exercise force' or as 'to be treated forcibly'. The latter translation implies Satan wars directly on the kingdom of God, putting Christ and us on the defensive.

Ladd argues that 'we do not discover [in the New Testament] the idea of Satan attacking the kingdom of God or exercising his power against the kingdom itself. *He can only wage his war against the sons of the kingdom . . . God is the aggressor; Satan is on the defensive*' (emphasis mine).[17] Ladd concludes that the best option is 'the kingdom of heaven "exercises its force" or "makes its way powerfully" in the world'.[18] *We* are thrust into the middle of a battle with Satan, a tug-of-war – the prize being the souls of men and women. Satan's captivity of men and women has many facets, denial of final salvation being his primary goal. But there are other types of dominion: bondage to sin, physical and emotional problems, social disruption, demonic affliction.

Our mission is to rescue those who have been taken captive as a result of Adam's fall. How we fulfil our mission is what the remainder of this book is about.

THE POWER ENCOUNTER

I was awakened late one night in 1978 by a desperate phone call. 'Please, Pastor Wimber, come and help Melinda' a young man cried into the telephone. He went on to explain that his friend, Melinda (not her real name), was in a pick-up truck in a nearby field. Eighteen years old and 100 pounds, she was thrashing about so violently that the truck was rocking. Strange sounds – not her normal voice – were coming from her: growling, animal-like sounds.

I was to meet a demon.

Before that I had believed in the existence of demons and probably even met a few without knowing it. But this was the first time I met one who was openly manifesting all of its evil, lying, and foul deeds through another human being. This was a pastoral call that I would never forget.

After arriving at the gas station, the boy took me to the truck. The girl (rather, something in the girl) spoke. 'I know you', were the first words to assault me – packaged in a hoarse, eerie voice – 'and you don't know what you're doing'.

I thought, 'You're right'.

The demon then said through Melinda, 'You can't do anything with her. She's mine'.

I thought, 'You're wrong'.

Then began ten hours of spiritual warfare with me calling on the forces of heaven to overcome Satan. During this time I had to endure putrid odours, eyes rolling back, profuse perspiration, blasphemy, and wild physical activity that required more strength than a petite girl operating under her own power could possibly possess. I was appalled, and very afraid.

But I refused to give up the fight.

In the end I think the demon left because I wore him out, certainly not because I was skilled at casting out evil spirits. (Since that time I have learned much about this type of encounter. If I had known then what I know now, I am convinced the episode would not have taken longer than an hour.)[1]

Battle of the kingdoms

Encounters with demons have become a common experience for me. Missionary Alan Tippett calls these events *power encounters*, the clashing of the kingdom of God with the kingdom of Satan.[2] These conflicts, these clashes, may occur anywhere, anytime. The expulsion of demons is most dramatic, though power encounters are far from limited only to the demonic.

Any system or force that must be overcome in order for the gospel to be believed is cause for a power encounter. This is especially true regarding missions. C. Peter Wagner, professor of church growth at Fuller Theological Seminary in Pasadena, California, commenting on power encounters and evangelism among tribal groups, writes that 'a power encounter is a visible, practical demonstration that Jesus Christ is more powerful than the false gods or spirits worshipped or feared by a people group'.[3]

Jesus began his public ministry with a power encounter. Soon after his forty days of fasting and testing in the wilderness, he went throughout Galilee, proclaiming the gospel and calling the first disciples. Eventually he landed in Capernaum, where he attended a synagogue meeting. As was the tradition for visiting rabbis, Jesus taught the people.

The people were 'amazed at his teaching, because he taught them as one who had authority, not as the teachers of the law' (Mark 1:22). A demon possessed man cried out, 'What do you want with us, Jesus of Nazareth? Have you come to destroy us? I know who you are – the Holy One of God!' (verse 24).

Here was a clear challenge to the kingdom of God. How did Christ respond? He silenced the spirit, then called him out of the man. The people were impressed with his power: 'He even gives orders to evil spirits and they obey him'. That evening, in response to the morning's deliverance, a large crowd gathered near the place where he was staying, with him again driving out demons and 'heal[ing] many who had various diseases' (verse 34).

Probably the most dramatic illustration of this type of encounter in the Old Testament is found in 1 Kings 18, the story of Elijah on Mount Carmel confronting the 450 prophets of Baal. Here we see God's prophet encountering an impotent god, a graven image representing a religious system that Satan backed. After wicked King Ahab accused Elijah of causing trouble in Israel, Elijah challenged him to an open confrontation: my God versus your Baal – and whoever is left standing in the end is the True God. Ahab accepted.

Before all the people, the Lord overwhelmed Baal. During the confrontation Elijah taunted the false prophets regarding Baal's impotency: 'Shout louder! Surely he is a god! Perhaps he is deep in thought, or busy, or travelling. Maybe he is sleeping and must be awakened' (verse 27). Elijah was aggressive, full of zeal for God's authority, seizing the opportunity not only to defeat Satan but also to demonstrate the lordship of Yahweh.

The key to the entire episode was Elijah's obedience to doing what God told him. He was a servant of God. 'O Lord', he prayed, 'God of Abraham, Isaac and Israel, let it be known today that you are God in Israel and that I am your servant and have done all these things *at your command*' (verse 36, emphasis mine). After this prayer, the fire of God fell, proving his presence. God's servant was vindicated.

The response from the people was immediate: 'The Lord, he is God! The Lord – he is God!'

Among primitive peoples there is the need to see the superior power of the gospel demonstrated for them to believe. C. Peter Wagner received this account from Terrie L. Lillie, a student who documented this report from a village in Kenya. It is told by an eyewitness whose primary language is not English:

A child was deadly sick in the same house after the end of the second week. She had malaria and surely she was dying. We were awakened at night by a big cry. We all ran to the direction of my grandmother's house. Kavili was crying, and Mbulu and the old woman. Kanini, the child born recently, was dying. She had changed her colour and her eyes had turned completely white. There was no blinking.

Many more people were there and a lot more were coming. I got inside. Here was the people who did not know what to do and how to do it. I was as they were, in the middle of the night, with no car or anything which could help anyone. No medicine was available at that time. Something had to be done. I thought it would be a good idea to pray and see what we would do next.

I asked to be given the child. I put her in my arms and called my wife to come near. I told everyone to come in that we may pray for the dying child. They came in but some feared that the child was going to die and so they did not go inside the house with a dead child. Then I had all of them sit. I began to pray. I did not make a long prayer. I said very few words. I simply asked the Lord to heal the child in the name of Jesus. Then I gave the child back to the mother.

The moment I gave her back, she was well. She was now breathing. She began to cry, she was nursed and she was well. Everyone took time to praise the name of the Lord. I could not really understand what was happening but I felt the power of God proceed out of me, and for a moment I did not want to say a lot. This was a big issue which made everyone present wonder to see how the Lord worked so quickly.

As a result of this instance, the whole village became Christians.

In this case, fatal illness needed to be overcome to open up the villagers to faith in Christ.

Alan Tippett describes an event in southern Polynesia that again illustrates the need that many peoples have to see the superior power of God demonstrated. So deeply ingrained is this reflex that a simple bump on a priestess's head releases them from years of bondage and fear to the false god Haehaetahi. Like Baal, Haehaetahi represented a religious system controlled by Satan:

Peter Vi [a missionary] worked with the chief, teaching him the gospel. Eventually the chief, Taufa'ahau, reached the point where he felt he must begin to worship God. This demanded a dynamic encounter or confrontation with his old god, Haehaetahi.

The priestess who served this god was much feared because she herself became the shrine of the deity under possession [of demons]. Taufa'ahau pulled a young banana tree and cut a club from the soft stalk. 'I will strike the devil-god with this,' he declared. On Vi's advice he removed the harder part of the root lest he kill the woman when he smote her under possession. At the moment when the priestess, under possession, was drinking the ceremonial kava, the chief struck her a blow on the forehead, which sent her rolling on the floor. Then before the drinking god had time to recover the chief struck again, and shouted a cry of victory that the god had been clubbed while drinking kava.[4]

The priestess was humiliated, losing her power. The people saw the victorious power of God, superior to the false god's power that had held them in fear and bondage. Because of this power encounter, they believed the gospel.

A war zone

An analogy that may help us understand what I mean by power encounter is found in nature. When warm and cold fronts collide, violence ensues: thunder and lightning, rain or snow – even tornadoes or hurricanes. There is conflict, and a resulting release of power. It is disorderly, messy – difficult to control.

Power encounters are much like that. When the kingdom of God comes into direct contact with the kingdom of the world (Jesus meets Satan) there is conflict. And usually it too is disorderly, messy – difficult for us to control.

The greatest instance of this is the crucifixion of Christ. At that moment an eternal sacrifice was made for us, so that the guilt of our sin might be forgiven, and the flesh, the world, and the Devil might be utterly defeated.

There was great power released that day. All of creation was rocked: the earth shook, rocks split, the sun stopped shining for three hours, the Temple curtain was torn in two. Even tombs were opened, releasing the dead – 'holy people', as they are described in Matthew 27:52. Life was radiating from the death of Christ; it shook a creation that was under the reign of evil.

Two fronts, two kingdoms, two economies had hit head on. And in the resurrection and ascension, Christ came out the victor, Satan the loser.

It was in this, the ultimate power encounter, that salvation was secured for all men and women who place their faith in Christ. But working that salvation out is another matter. In the present age, an interim period, before the coming of the fullness of the kingdom, the victory over Satan needs to be applied in the lives of people still under his power.

Many Christians do not adequately recognise that though Christ's victory is irreversible, its application to everyday events is ongoing. Satan is still alive and well, even though his time on earth is limited.

German theologian Oscar Cullmann offers an analogy that helps us understand how, though defeated, Satan still has great power – power that can kill if left unchecked. In World War II, most military experts agree, victory for the Allies was assured on D-Day (June 6, 1944), the day they successfully invaded Nazi occupied Europe on the Normandy beaches. Because Germany failed to prevent their entrance, victory for the British, American, and Canadian forces was inevitable.

But it took eleven months for the Allies to actually end the war. During this time thousands of men lost their lives in the bloodiest battles of the entire conflict. The coming V-E Day (May 8, 1945) was assured but not realised.[5]

We are in a similar position as Christians: the final and full establishment of the kingdom of God, with Christ as its head, was assured at the resurrection. But we have yet to realise its fullness in the days in which we live.

We too are soldiers, members of Christ's army. In 2 Timothy 2:3 Paul instructs Timothy, 'Endure hardship with us like a good soldier of Christ Jesus'. There is a war yet to be fought, an enemy still capable of inflicting great harm – if we allow him to.

One nation, one language

The unity of the early Christians was a crucial ingredient for their experiencing the power of the Spirit. In the book of Acts, when Christians are described as being together in heart and mind, the power of God comes in extraordinary measure:

*They were 'together in one place' (2:1), and Pentecost happened (2:2–13).
*They 'devoted themselves to the apostles' teaching and to the fellowship' (2:42), and 'many wonders and miraculous signs were done' (2:43).
*They 'were one in heart and mind' (4:32), and 'With great power the apostles continued to testify' (4:33).

In the second chapter we read of the birth of a warrior nation, the army of God, the church. In this nation we discover God's response to man's earlier attempt to unify as 'one people speaking the same language' at the Tower of Babel (Genesis 11:1–9). Against the backdrop of man's failure at Babel we learn a spiritual principle of unity from God's victory at Pentecost.

At Babel, while observing the nations attempt to make a name for themselves, the Lord said, 'If as one people speaking the same language they have begun to do this, *then nothing they plan to do will be impossible* for them. Come, let us go down and confuse their language so they will not understand each other' (emphasis mine).

God readily acknowledges that power is present when people are united in purpose and language. Even the most rebellious and selfish people, when they come together, can accomplish much of what they set out to do. The potential for good *and evil* within men and women is almost boundless when they cooperate.

At Pentecost the Holy Spirit came to create a new nation from many nations, a new race from many races – the people of God (Acts 2:5–6, 41). There are several words used in scripture to convey the meaning of a Christian nation. One of the most common Greek words for nation is *ethnos*. Karl Ludwig Schmidt, in the *Theological Dictionary of the New Testament*, says *ethnos* means a 'multitude bound by the same manners, customs, or other distinctive features. It gives us the sense of people'.[6] If the 'nations' of the world are always referred to as many, the 'nation' of Christ is singular, a unit. This means that though a multitude, we are viewed by God as one people or society (see 1 Peter 2:10; Gal. 3:6–9). This unity is one key to experiencing spiritual power.

One nation needs one language. At Pentecost God created order out of confusion, understanding of his word out of a multitude of languages. When the Holy Spirit came on the disciples, all present heard them speak in their native tongues. Scripture describes their initial response as being 'amazed and perplexed' (Acts 2:12). This was all the more remarkable because the disciples were uneducated. (As Galileans, the disciples had heavy accents. Though not expressly stated in the text, I believe that the disciples not only spoke other people's languages but also their accents. This would be akin to someone with a thick Liverpool or Alabama accent speaking flawless Parisian French. Truly this would be a miracle.)

At Babel, one nation was broken into many, one language thrown into confusion – resulting in a loss of power and purpose. At Pentecost, many nations and tongues were unified – and they were able to experience an outpouring of power and the addition of 3,000 new disciples (Acts 2:41).

Often a power encounter that leads to conversion occurs first in those who are evangelising, then in those who are evangelised. People at Pentecost were 'amazed and perplexed'. Many of them, though, took a quick step, crossing over to the other side: they became participants in God's grace. A power encounter in a Christian, when witnessed by non-Christians, will supernaturally open them to the gospel of the kingdom of God.

It took Peter's explanation of the phenomenon to lead the 3,000 to Christ. Usually, when a power encounter is witnessed by non-Christians, they have many questions that only the gospel can answer. A rational explanation must be added to a transrational experience, the natural to the supernatural, for the most forceful advance of the kingdom of God.

An international army was born from the Pentecost power encounter. The remainder of Acts reads like war chronicles, with God's army doing his bidding. Our lives should read the same way.

Christians too

Power encounters are difficult to control.

This is a hard word for many Western Christians to accept, because phenomena that do not fit rational thought are uncomfortable: they plunge us into the murky world of the transrational in which we lose control of the situation. Events that do not fit our normal categories of thinking are threatening for us, causing fear, because they are unfamiliar – especially where spiritual power is involved.

The first time I experienced a power encounter similar to the one described at Pentecost, I became extremely irritated, angry at God. It was Mother's Day, 1979, and I had invited a young man to speak at the evening service of the church that I had only recently begun to pastor, the Vineyard Christian Fellowship in Anaheim, California. He came out of the California 'Jesus people' movement of the late 60s and early 70s, and (so I heard) was unpredictable when he spoke. I was apprehensive about him, but sensed God wanted him to speak nevertheless. He had been used by God to lead Christians into a refreshing experience of the Holy Spirit, and it was obvious to me that the congregation needed spiritual renewal. I hasten to point out that asking this young man to speak went contrary to my normal instincts as a pastor. I took seriously the admonition that pastors are to protect their flocks. But in this instance I sensed it was what God wanted. Regardless, I was to stand by the decision, whatever the cost.

When he eagerly agreed to speak, I became even more apprehensive. What will he say? What will he do to my church? The Lord gently reminded me, 'Whose church is this?'

That evening he gave his testimony, a powerful story of God's grace. As he spoke, I relaxed. Nothing strange here, I thought.

Then he did something that I had never seen done in a church gathering. He finished his talk and said, 'Well, that's my testimony. Now the church has been offending the Holy Spirit a long time and he is quenched. So we are going to invite him to come and minister'. We all waited. The air became thick with anticipation – and anxiety.

Then he said, 'Holy Spirit, come'. And he did!

(I must remind you that we were not a 'Pentecostal' church with experience or understanding of the sorts of things that began to happen. What happened could not have been learned behaviour.)

People fell to the floor. Others, who did not believe in tongues, loudly spoke in tongues. The speaker roamed among the crowd, praying for people who then immediately fell over, with the Holy Spirit resting on them.

I was aghast! All I could think throughout this time was 'Oh,

God, get me out of here.' In the aftermath, we lost church members and my staff were extremely upset. That night I could not sleep. Instead, I spent the evening reading scripture, looking for the verse, 'Holy Spirit, come.' I never found it.

By 4:30 a.m. I was more upset than I was earlier at the meeting. Then I remembered that I had read in *The Journal of John Wesley* where something like this had happened. I went out to my garage and found a box of books about revivals and revivalists and began to read them. What I discovered was that our experience at the Vineyard Christian Fellowship was not unique; people like John and Charles Wesley, George Whitefield, Charles Finney, and Jonathan Edwards all had similar phenomena in their ministries. By 6:00 a.m. I had found at least ten examples of similar phenomena in church history.[7]

For example, on May 24th, 1739, John Wesley wrote in his journal:

> Mr. Hall, Hinching, Ingham, Whitefield, Hutching and my brother Charles were present at our love feast in Fetter Lane with about 60 of our brethren. About three in the morning as we were continuing instant in prayer the power of God came mightly upon us, insomuch that many cried out for exulting joy and many fell to the ground. As soon as we were recovered a little from the awe and amazement at the presence of his Majesty, we broke out with one voice, 'We praise thee O God, we acknowledge thee to be the Lord.'

Then I asked God for assurance that this was from him, that this was something he – not man or Satan – was doing. Just after praying this prayer, the phone rang. Tom Stipe, a Denver, Colorado, pastor, and good friend, called. I told him what had happened the night before, and he responded that it was from God. 'That's exactly what happened in the early days of the Jesus People revival. Many people were saved'.

That conversation was significant, because Tom was a credible witness. I had only heard about these things; Tom had lived through them.

Over the next few months, supernatural phenomena continued to occur, frequently uninvited and without any encouragement. They happened spontaneously. New life came into our church. Every person who was touched by and yielded to the Holy Spirit – whether they fell over, started shaking, became very quiet and still, or spoke in tongues – accepted the experience and thought it was wonderful, drawing them closer to God. More importantly, prayer, scripture reading, caring for others, and the love of God all increased.[8]

Our young people began roaming the community, looking for people to evangelise and pray over. An event that I heard about is a good illustration of what often happened. One day a group of our young people approached a stranger in a parking lot. Soon they were praying over him, and he fell to the ground. By the time he got up, the stranger was converted. He is now a member of our church.

A revival broke out that May, and by September we had baptised over 700 new converts. There may have been as many as 1,700 new converts during a three-and-one-half month period. I was an expert on church growth, but I had never seen evangelism like that.

Power encounters in the church, in this case against 'civilised propriety', catapulted us into all-out revival. What I had thought of as 'order' in the twentieth century church evidently was not the same as what Christians experienced in the New Testament church.

There is a word of caution, though. We would be mistaken to think that lack of order or organisation allows the Holy Spirit greater freedom to work, while more order inhibits him. The right kind of order is necessary for the church to develop to maturity and fulfil its tasks. The church is an organism, a living body. A corpse is highly organised, but it is dead – it has no spirit within it. Many congregations are like corpses: well-ordered but lacking the life of Christ. On the other hand, the one-celled amoeba, which certainly lacks organisation and complexity, may have life but can accomplish little. Prayer groups and other Christian organisations that reject the need for leadership are often like amoebas: having life but not able to accomplish much.

What God wants is a living body, where the Holy Spirit is free to operate and the body is ordered in such a manner that it can accomplish much. This body is quite complex, because the goal of evangelism and discipleship is an involved process. A key, though, is that God's order – not our own – be established. Sometimes he tips over our order so he can establish his.

Fearing God's power

In Acts 5:12–16 we read of another response to power encounters: fear. 'The apostles performed many miraculous signs and wonders among the people', this passage begins. In Jerusalem the apostles met daily at Solomon's Colonnade in the Temple, and the power of God came. At this time they were 'highly regarded by the people'.

But the disciples were also feared, feared because people knew God was with them. 'No one else dared join them', scripture says.

Today, many churches have become so secularised – even profane – that the community has no thought or concern about entering their premises. In fact, the world often sees the church as only another organisation in need of their help. I frequently receive letters from secular fundraising organisations offering to raise money for our church. For many, the church is an ineffective institution in need of expert advice – for a fee, of course.

In the New Testament, outsiders were afraid because they did not know what would happen to them if they moved in among Christians. They could be consumed by God's power; their secret sins could be revealed; healing could come on them; demons could be expulsed. Paul, writing to the Corinthians concerning the proper ordering of the gifts, instructs them to expect power evangelism:

> So if the whole church comes together and everyone speaks in tongues, and some who do not understand or some unbelievers come in, will they not say that you are out of your mind? But if an unbeliever or someone who does not understand comes in while everybody is prophesying, he will be convinced by all that he is a sinner and will be judged by all, and the secrets of his heart will be laid bare. So he will fall down and worship God, exclaiming, 'God is really among you!' (1 Corinthians 14:23–25)

God's Spirit works this way today. I recently read this anonymous account of a homosexual's conversion experience:

> One weekend I went to visit some friends outside the city [in which he lived], people I knew from before my openly homosexual days. We had taken quite different directions –

they were now Christians involved in the charismatic renewal – and I had never told them about my new life. However, I
still enjoyed seeing them occasionally. In fact I was in-
trigued by their visible joy and fervor.

During this particular visit they asked me to go with them
to a prayer meeting. I agreed, even though I expected an
hour and a half of boredom. We drove through the steamy
summer night to a large room crowded with people.

The meeting began with a few words from the leader and a
couple of songs, followed by the low murmur of people
praying aloud. It seemed things had barely begun when the
leader was back on his feet, looking a little nervous. I can
still hear him saying, 'The Lord has told me that someone
here tonight has been practicing homosexuality. He wants
you to know that he loves you and forgives you.'

That gentle message hit me like a thunderbolt. For years I
had pushed the God of my childhood out of my mind. Now
God was speaking to me. He wasn't just saying hello, either:
he was asking me to give up my whole way of life.

I spent the rest of the meeting fighting with myself. 'Why
do I need forgiveness?' I would think. 'I haven't done
anything wrong.' Then the religion lessons of my early years
would come rushing back: who God was, what it meant that
he loved me, what it meant to reject him. In the end, my
debate boiled down to this: 'I know enough about God to
know that if he is speaking to me – and I believe he is – the
only sensible thing for me to do is obey.'

When the meeting ended, I turned to my friends. 'That
message was for me,' I told them. 'I want to do what God
says.'

. . . Eventually I felt ready for marriage and fell in love
with the woman who is now my wife. Our life together has
been my most constant source of happiness.[9]

My co-author, Kevin Springer, met the author of this testimony. Eight years after writing these words, he is still a strong
Christian. He and his wife have three beautiful children. Reflecting on his conversion experience, he said, 'For years before my
conversion I was nervous around charismatics, uneasy that God
might reveal my homosexuality to them. But by the time I

attended the meeting in which I was converted, I was no longer on guard. So right when I let my guard down, God's power came on me'.

Overcoming opposition

In the thirteenth chapter of Acts we find a power encounter similar to the one between Elijah and the prophets of Baal. Paul and Barnabas, recently sent from the church at Antioch, were in the city of Paphos, on the island of Cyprus. Word of their presence had come to Sergius Paulus, the Roman proconsul, and he sent for them 'because he wanted to hear the word of God'.

The scene is set for encounter between light and dark when Paul and Barnabas enter Sergius Paulus's chamber. Present was Elymas the sorcerer, opposing them with the purpose of turning the proconsul from his emerging faith. Jesus had his witness, Paul, and Satan his, Elymas.

There was need for action if Sergius Paulus was to be fully converted. Paul, filled with the Holy Spirit, took up the challenge. He said to Elymas, 'You are a child of the devil and an enemy of everything that is right! You are full of all kinds of deceit and trickery . . . Now the hand of the Lord is against you. You are going to be blind, and for a time you will be unable to see the light of the sun', At that moment Paul was speaking the words of God, under his unction. Elymas was immediately blinded.

And Sergius Paulus believed. Why? Because 'he was amazed at the teaching about the Lord'. What was the teaching? That the Lord was present, and was more powerful than anything in creation.

Note that in this instance the power encounter centred in Elymas, the enemy of God. The response of those present was faith in God. They heard *and saw* the presence of the kingdom of heaven demonstrated.

Overcoming nature

Sometimes even nature can have a power encounter, resulting in great fear and openness among all present. When Paul and Silas were thrown into the Philippian prison (they had been falsely accused of inciting an uproar) God's power struck the prison, causing an earthquake, opening the doors, and loosening their chains (see Acts 16:16–40).

The jailer, who had fallen asleep, assumed the prisoners had fled. Roman guards who for any reason allowed their prisoners to escape were killed. So the jailer drew his sword to take his own life. But Paul stopped him. 'Don't harm yourself! We are all here'!

Paul's response to God's power was mercy, mercy extended to the jailer. Instead of fleeing for their own lives, Paul and Silas stayed in the prison. The jailer rushed to them, falling down and asking, 'What must I do to be saved'? Paul replied, 'Believe in the Lord Jesus, and you will be saved'. The jailer and his household were saved, 'and the whole family was filled with joy, because they had come to believe in God'. When God's power is combined with his mercy, fearful hearts melt.

The great commission

We should not be surprised that the book of Acts is full of stories like these. At the end of Matthew's gospel, Jesus commissioned us to be sources of power encounters, ever ready to seize any opportunity to proclaim God's grace and mercy in order to make fully trained and obedient disciples. I believe the great commission can be fulfilled more effectively as we open our lives to God's power in the ways that I speak of in this book.

Before commanding us to 'go and make disciples of all nations', Jesus prefaced his words with the statement: 'All authority in heaven and on earth has been given to me'. *All* authority is in Christ, so anything that he commands us to do, we have access to the power required to do it.

The Greek word used here for authority is *exousia*. Theologian Werner Foerster notes that this word 'denotes [Jesus'] divinely given power and authority to act . . . It is his own rule in free agreement with the Father'.[10] The Lord's prayer to the Father was that 'your kingdom come, your will be done on earth as it is in heaven' (Matthew 6:10). Jesus' entire life was built on the principle of doing the will of the Father, walking in his works. 'I tell you the truth', he told the Jews who were persecuting him, 'the Son can do nothing by himself; he can do only what he sees his Father doing, because whatever the Father does the Son also does' (John 5:19).

All authority for making disciples is found in Christ, and he is with us today. 'Surely I will be with you always, to the very end of the age', he assures us in the great commission (Matthew 28:20).

How is he with us? 'All that belongs to the Father is mine. That is why I said the Spirit will take from what is mine and make it known to you' (John 16:15). It is the Holy Spirit, the 'go-between God', who holds the key to power encounters. Our openness and availability to his direction and enabling, anointing and power, are the catalyst for fulfilling the great commission.

Clearly the early Christians had an openness to power encounters, which resulted in signs and wonders and church growth. If we want to be like the early church, we too need to open to the Holy Spirit's power.

3

POWER EVANGELISM

It was the end of a long day of ministry, and I was exhausted. I had just completed a teaching conference in Chicago and was flying off to another speaking engagement in New York. I was looking forward to the plane ride as a chance to relax for a few hours before plunging back into teaching.

But it was not to be the quiet, uneventful trip I had hoped for.

Shortly after take-off, I pushed back the reclining seat and readjusted the seat belt, preparing to relax. My eyes wandered around the cabin, not looking at anything in particular. Seated across the aisle from me was a middle-aged man: a business man, to judge from his appearance, nothing unusual or noteworthy about him. But in the split-second that my eyes happened to be cast in his direction, I saw something that startled me.

Written across his face, in very clear and distinct letters, I thought I saw the word 'adultery'. I blinked, rubbed my eyes, and looked again. It was still there. 'Adultery'. I was seeing it, not with my natural eyes, but in my mind's eye. No one else on the plane, I am sure, saw it. It was the Spirit of God communicating to me. The fact that it was a spiritual reality made it no less real.

By now the man had become aware that I was looking at him ('gaping at him' might be a more accurate description).

'What do you want' he snapped.

As he spoke, a woman's name came clearly to mind. This was more familiar to me; I had become accustomed to the Holy Spirit bringing things to my awareness through these kinds of promptings.

Somewhat nervously, I leaned across the aisle and asked,

'Does the name Jane [not her real name] mean anything to you'?

His face turned ashen. 'We've got to talk', he stammered.

The plane we were on was a jumbo jet, the kind with a small upstairs cocktail lounge. As I followed him up the stairs to the lounge, I sensed the Spirit speaking to me yet again. 'Tell him if he doesn't turn from his adultery, I'm going to take him'.

Terrific. All I had wanted was a nice, peaceful plane ride to New York. Now here I was, sitting in an aeroplane cocktail lounge with a man I had never seen before, whose name I didn't even know, about to tell him God was going to take his life if he didn't stop his affair with some woman.

We sat down in strained silence. He looked at me suspiciously for a moment, then asked, 'Who told you that name'?

'God told me', I blurted out. I was too rattled to think of a way to ease into the topic more gracefully.

'*God* told you'? He almost shouted the question, he was so shocked by what I had said.

'Yes', I answered, taking a deep breath. 'He also told me to tell you . . . that unless you turn from this adulterous relationship, he is going to take your life'.

I braced myself for what I was sure would be an angry, defensive reaction. But to my relief, the instant I spoke to him his defensiveness crumbled and his heart melted. In a choked, desperate voice he asked me, 'What should I do'?

At last I was back on familiar ground. I explained to him what it meant to repent and trust Christ, and invited him to pray with me. With hands folded and head bowed, I began to lead him in a quiet prayer: 'O God . . .'

That was as far as I got. The conviction of sin that had built up inside him seemed virtually to explode. Bursting into tears, he cried out, 'O *God*, I'm so *sorry* . . .' and launched into the most heart-rending repentance I had ever heard.

It was impossible, in such cramped quarters, to keep hidden what was happening. Before long everyone in the cocktail lounge was intimately acquainted with this man's past sinfulness and present contrition. Even the stewardesses were weeping right along with him!

When he finished praying and regained his composure, we talked for a while about what had happened to him.

'The reason I was so upset when you first mentioned that name to me', he explained, 'was that my wife was sitting in the seat right next to me. I didn't want her to hear'.

I knew he wasn't going to like what I said to him next.

'You're going to have to tell her'.

'I am'? he responded weakly. 'When'?

'Better do it right now', I said gently.

The prospect of confessing to his wife was, understandably, somewhat intimidating, but he could see there was no other way. So again I followed him, down the stairs and back to our seats.

I couldn't hear the conversation over the noise of the plane, but I could see his wife's stunned reaction, not only to his confession of infidelity, but also to his account of how the stranger sitting across the aisle had been sent by God to warn him of the consequences of his sin. Eyes wide with amazement (and probably terror!), she stared first at her husband, then at me, then back at her husband, then back at me, as the amazing story unfolded. In the end the man led his wife to accept Christ, right there on the aeroplane.

There was little time to talk when we got off the aeroplane in New York. They didn't own a Bible, so I gave them mine. Then we went our separate ways.

This might seem like an unusual – if not bizarre – event, yet I could write hundreds of other accounts like it – both from my own experience and from that of others whom I know. I call this type of encounter *power evangelism*, and, I believe, it was one of the most effective means of evangelism in the early church.[1] Further, power evangelism appears to be present during periods of great missionary expansion and renewal throughout church history (see Appendix A).

By power evangelism I mean a presentation of the gospel that is rational but also transcends the rational. The explanation of the gospel comes with a demonstration of God's power through signs and wonders. Power evangelism is a spontaneous, Spirit-inspired, empowered presentation of the gospel. Power evangelism is that evangelism which is preceded and undergirded by supernatural demonstrations of God's presence.

Through these supernatural encounters people experience the presence and power of God. Usually this occurs in words of knowledge (such as the man on the aeroplane experienced), healing, prophecy, and deliverance from evil spirits. In power evangelism, resistance to the gospel is supernaturally overcome, and receptivity to Christ's claims is usually very high.

Many of us are suspicious of a story in which supernatural knowledge of personal sin is used in evangelism. This demonstrates how far Christianity in Western society has drifted from experiences that were everyday occurrences in New Testament times. Yet if power evangelism is a normal type of evangelism, and Western Christians rarely experience it, this exclusion will be reflected in the results of our evangelistic efforts.

Who is evangelising whom?

Are the Christian churches effective in evangelism today? Jesus told his disciples, 'The harvest is plentiful but the workers are few' (Matthew 9:37). In the West the number of workers in domestic (and foreign) missions has been increasing for the past fifteen years, especially among evangelicals. (We would be mistaken to think that only missionaries or full-time Christian leaders are the 'workers' Christ was calling for in the ninth chapter of Matthew. *Every* Christian has been called to the harvest. However, numerical increases of professional workers without a corresponding increase in the harvest indicates that there is another factor responsible for the waning of Christianity in Western culture.)

English and American domestic missionary organisations such as Campus Crusade for Christ, the Navigators, Inter-Varsity Christian Fellowship, and countless evangelical denominational groups are more active now than at any time in their history. Programmes like Evangelism Explosion, Luis Palau Crusades, and Campus Crusade's 'Here's Life' have growing staffs. Though there is always a need for more workers, there has never been a time in this century when so many workers and programmes have been tilling the fields.

Taking into consideration the increase in domestic missionary activity in recent years, one would expect an improved church life. One indicator of the level of church life (and indirectly the effectiveness of evangelisation efforts) is church attendance. In England less than ten percent of the population are weekly church attenders. In the United States – a country not as secularised as England – church participation is much higher.

Currently, forty-two percent of the US population attend a worship service in a typical week, and sixty-eight percent are enrolled in the churches (140,816,358 people reported in 1984). These numbers nevertheless represent a steady downward trend in attendance over the past fifteen years.[2]

More significantly, those who claim to be Christians are not living effective, fully converted lives. Commenting on the problem, author Joseph Bayly notes, 'I don't think any observer would dispute the fact that the evangelical Protestant subculture has been overrun by the general American culture's values. If divorce rates have risen in the general culture, they have also risen among evangelical Protestants . . . [They] follow a similar pattern of TV viewing, of materialism, and other cultural changes'.[3] In fact, according to recent studies conducted by the National Opinion Research Center, the percentage of those married who have been divorced or legally separated is higher among US Protestants than in the general population.[4]

George Gallup, in his report, '1984 Religion in America', was more stinging in his observation of the level of Christian living in the United States: 'Religion is growing in importance among Americans but morality is losing ground . . . There is very little difference in the behaviour of the churched and unchurched on a wide range of items including lying, cheating, and pilferage'.

There could be other explanations for these discouraging figures and observations. For example, they could also indicate that the world is more effectively evangelising Christians than we are evangelising the world. In other words, the figures could point more to secularisation trends within the church, which is not necessarily an indictment on our missionary methods.

More significantly, these figures could also indicate that there are problems not with the methods so much as with the message: a 'cheap-grace' gospel is frequently preached, producing weak Christians who do not stand when powerful and persuasive attacks come from the world. I believe this is a serious problem; many Christians do not understand or know how to communicate the gospel of the kingdom of God.

I am not implying that all Western, evangelical methods of evangelism are ineffective. Denominations, like the Christian and Missionary Alliance, the Church of the Nazarine, and the Southern Baptists, which generally oppose the charismatic gifts, have experienced impressive growth in recent years. But on a worldwide scale, an estimated 70 percent of all church growth is among Pentecostal and charismatic groups.

Better indicators of the effectiveness of Western, evangelical methodologies are studies of specific programmes. Dr. Win Arn, writing in the January–February 1977 issue of *Church Growth America*, reported on several programmes, including Campus Crusade for Christ's 'Here's Life America' – a media and phone contact programme. Of the West Morris Street Free Methodist Church in Indianapolis, Indiana, whose church participated in a 'Here's Life' campaign, Dr. Arn wrote: 'In researching the facts with Pastor Riggs we found . . . that the church made over 6,000 phone calls . . . 362 people made a decision . . . 20 attended one or more Bible studies. When I asked how many of those who had made decisions were now (five months later) members of the church, the answer was "Zero". Effective evangelism? Hardly'.

Peter Wagner, writing in the September 1977 issue of *Eternity* magazine, offers even more conclusive figures on the 'Here's Life America' programme. He gathered data from 178 participating churches in six cities. These are the results:

26,535 gospels presented
 4,106 decisions for Christ
   526 came to a Bible study
   125 new church members

While the 4,106 figure is impressive, the people do not appear to be fully converted. They lack the convincing fruit of discipleship in their lives: they do not go on with Bible study and church membership, both reliable indicators of effective evangelism.

In the January–February 1978 issue of *Church Growth America*, Dr. Arn reported on results from the 1976 Seattle-Tacoma Billy Graham Crusade. Here are his figures:

434,100 persons attended
 18,000 decisions were registered (4.2 percent)
  9,739 were rededications (2.2 percent)
  5,550 were for salvation (1.3 percent)
  2,847 were unknown responses (0.7 percent)
  1,285 were incorporated into a local church (0.29 percent)

While these statistics are more encouraging than those for

'Here's Life America', they still do not indicate effective evangelism.

Both Billy Graham and Campus Crusade for Christ are aware of these statistics, and they have taken steps to improve on them. For example, Eddie Gibbs, a professor at Fuller Seminary, helped develop a follow-up programme to Billy Graham's 1984 England Crusade, and early statistics indicate a much higher percentage of people are joining local churches and Bible studies than in previous Crusades. Campus Crusade now employs men and women trained in principles of church growth developed by Donald McGavran and C. Peter Wagner.

Most evangelism practised in the West lacks the power seen in New Testament evangelism. Although there is always a need for more workers to reap the harvest, the current situation in Western societies indicates a need also for more powerful ways of reaching people with the gospel.

It's a Western problem

You will notice that I said that the need for effective evangelism is greatest in Western societies; in many non-Western (usually third-world) countries, this does not appear to be the case. C. Peter Wagner was a missionary in Bolivia for sixteen years. Here is what he learned about growing churches in Latin societies:

> My background is that of a Scofield Bible dispensational evangelical. I was taught that the gifts of the Spirit were not in operation in our age; they went out with the apostolic church . . . [Even today] I see myself neither a charismatic nor a Pentecostal . . . I began looking around and trying to get a handle on church growth in Latin America. Much to my surprise I began discovering that the churches that were far outgrowing all the others were the Pentecostal churches.
>
> While I lived in Bolivia I travelled quite a bit to Chile and studied the Pentecostal movement there. The understanding I got through the Chilean Pentecostals began to open me to the validity of signs, wonders, healings, and tongues in our day and age.

His conclusion regarding the key to effective evangelism is remarkable, especially when it is kept in mind that Dr. Wagner is not a 'classical' Pentecostal:

> What I'm seeing, as the picture is beginning to emerge, is that worldwide there is a remarkably close relationship between growth of the churches today and the healing ministry – particularly, but not exclusively, in new areas where the gospel has just penetrated, where the devil has had complete reign for centuries or millennia. When the gospel first penetrates a region, if we don't go in with an understanding of and use of the supernatural power of the Holy Spirit, we just don't make much headway . . .
>
> [For example,] in Brazil 40 percent of the population are practising spiritists and another 40 percent have had some direct experience with it. The way the gospel is spreading there is by a confrontation: healings, miracles, signs, and wonders.[5]

Another example of what Dr. Wagner describes is the Full Gospel Central Church, located in Seoul, Korea. Launched on May 18, 1958, under the direction of Dr. Paul Yonggi Cho, the church today has over 500,000 members, with 17,000 members being added each month! It is unquestionably the world's largest local church.

'My mind drifts back to the beginning days of the church, known even then for a constant flow of God's miracle power', says Dr. John Hurston, who has been with the Full Gospel Central Church since its beginning. He was responding to a question about the reason for its phenomenal growth: 'Perhaps the answer . . . is the continuation of a trend modelled by Christ: "People brought to Jesus many who had demons in them. Jesus drove out the evil spirits with a word and healed all who were sick" (Matthew 8:16)'.

Power evangelism is flourishing in non-technological countries. People living in these countries are often animists – that is, they believe there are actual spirits that hold people in bondage and the supernatural power of the Holy Spirit is needed to break their hold. A colleague of mine from Fuller Theological Seminary, Dr. Charles Kraft, tells about going to Nigeria and attempting to teach the book of Romans to a small tribe. After a few months, they came to him, very politely, and said that they appreciated his teaching but it was not relevant to their needs. What they needed was wisdom for dealing with spirits that plagued the villagers every night, something that Kraft readily admitted he was not trained to do.

Under such circumstances it is not surprising that most Western missionary organisations report that approximately half of their foreign missionaries return home after only one tour of duty.[6]

We would be mistaken if we thought that power evangelism was needed only in countries with more primitive (less technological) cultures. In Western culture, because of the influence of materialism and rationalism, many people do not believe in a spirit world, or if they do, they do not believe or live as though the spirit world can affect the material world. But their unbelief does not exclude demonic activity from our societies; a demon's existence is not dependent on our belief in him. A mindset that excludes the possibility of direct intervention by supernatural powers (good or bad) in the world makes Christians vulnerable to Satan.

Because Western Christians are inhibited from practising power evangelism their effectiveness is blunted. This leaves them ineffective in dealing with people who have problems with demons, illness and serious sin.

In 1974 I resigned as co-pastor of Yorba Linda Friends Church to become founding head of the Department of Church Growth at what is now called the Charles E. Fuller Institute of Evangelism and Church Growth in Pasadena, California. At the same time I began an adjunct professorship at the School of World Missions–Institute of Church Growth, Fuller Theological Seminary. Working with men like Donald A. McGavran (who is recognised worldwide as the father of the church growth movement), C. Peter Wagner, Charles Kraft, I became familiar with the practice of power evangelism in third-world countries, particularly with reports of signs and wonders and dramatic church growth. These reports caught my attention.

At the same time I travelled extensively across the United States, in a four-year period working with over 40,000 pastors from twenty-seven denominations (none Pentecostal or charismatic), speaking about church growth and evangelism. The contrast between churches on the mission field and in America was striking: American churches lacked both power encounters and dramatic growth so common in other parts of the world.

When I had left the pastorate in 1974 I thought I would never return. I could no longer lead an institution that I had many questions about. My subsequent travels around the country did little to change many of my negative impressions of American evangelical churches.

But in 1978 God spoke to me about returning to the pastorate. Through the credible, intelligent testimony of Pentecostal professors like Russell Spittler, through the reports of signs and wonders from third-world students and missionaries, and through a greater understanding of how Western materialism undermines Christians' acceptance of the supernatural, I had begun to open my heart to the Holy Spirit. I wondered, were signs and wonders and church growth like that experienced in third-world countries possible in the United States? I would have to become a pastor again to find out.

So, with much apprehension, and the encouragement of my wife and Peter Wagner, I resigned my position and returned to the pastorate, a wayward shepherd coming to serve a tiny flock. Unlike my first pastorate, this time I had a clear sense of mission: to prove whether the signs and wonders and church growth being reported by Fuller Seminary third-world students was possible in the United States.

We started with about fifty people, a home meeting in which we worshipped God, studied scripture, sang, and prayed. By our second year we had grown to over 200 members and were meeting in a high school gymnasium. (Later we took on the name Vineyard Christian Fellowship.) In our first year we did not experience the signs and wonders described in the New Testament. Therefore, I began a series of sermons from the gospel of Luke. Luke is full of the healing ministry of Jesus; I was forced to begin teaching on the subject. I thought, what better place to start than with the healing ministry?

Soon I was praying for the sick, not because I had seen the sick healed but because that was what scripture taught Christians to do. Over the course of the next ten months, week in and week out, I prayed for people – and not one person was healed. Half of the members left the church. I kept preaching and praying about healing because during this period (when I wanted to quit) God had spoken a clear word to me: 'Do not preach your experience. Preach my word'. Though I continued to sound foolish because of my lack of results, I did not stop preaching about God's desire to heal today. (I was not claiming that people were healed who in fact were not healed, only that based on the Bible, more people should be healed today.)

During this time the Lord taught me several things. First, it took months for me to realise that if an experience such as healing was commonly found in scripture yet not a part of my experience, something was wrong with how I approached it. Before, I had assumed that God didn't hear me.

I assumed that scripture study, especially as approached in evangelical seminaries, was the key to being equipped and empowered to do God's work. In fact, I was to learn, there was more to being equipped than learning about the Bible. I still believe in the importance and necessity for education but I no longer see it as the sole avenue to equipping and empowering.

Second, I became aware of different types of faith and how often I did not seek faith for miracles. As an evangelical I thought of personal Christian growth as having two components, doctrinal faith and faithfulness. Doctrinal faith comes as we grow in understanding right doctrine or correct teaching. We know that we are growing in doctrinal faith as we grow intellectually, in knowledge about God: his nature, character, how he acts, and so on. Faithfulness is character growth or the development of the fruit of the Spirit in our lives (Galatians 5:22–23) and essentially I found that to be true but incomplete.

Through this ten-month period I became aware of another dimension of Christian growth, an exercise of faith for miracles such as healing, words of knowledge, and so on. (Perhaps this is the 'faith' described in 1 Corinthians 12:9.) Key to this was learning how to know when God's unction or anointing had come for a task like healing in a particular situation.

Emphasis on doctrinal knowledge and character development is good; this other dimension of Christian growth adds much more. This was a difficult lesson for me to learn, which explains why nothing happened for many months.

At the end of this ten-month period, when I was at my lowest point, a woman was healed. Her husband had called, asking me to come and pray for her – she was very ill. The healing occurred after I prayed for her and had begun a well-rehearsed explanation to her husband about why she probably wouldn't be healed. During my explanation she got out of bed, completely whole again.

This began a trickle that soon became a steady stream.

Today we see hundreds of people healed every month in Vineyard Christian Fellowship services. Many more are healed as we pray for them in hospitals, on the streets, and in homes. The blind see; the lame walk; the deaf hear. Cancer is disappearing.

Most importantly for me as a pastor, the people are taking healing and other supernatural gifts to the streets, leading many who otherwise would not be open to the message of the gospel to Christ. I estimate that twenty percent of our people regularly see someone healed through their prayers. The gifts are not confined to church services; they are tools employed in reaching the lost.

D. Martyn Lloyd-Jones, in a book taken from sermons, *Joy Unspeakable*, points out that in the book of Acts the relationship between the anointing of the Holy Spirit and evangelism is striking: 'Go through Acts and in every instance when we are told either that the Spirit came upon these men or that they were filled with the Spirit, you will find that it was in order to bear a witness and a testimony.'[7]

Since 1978 the Vineyard Christian Fellowships have grown to include 120 congregations, mostly in the United States and England, with over 32,000 members. The majority of our members are new converts (mostly young people) who have experienced a power encounter.

Vineyard Christian Fellowships are not the only churches that have discovered power evangelism. Others like St. Andrews Anglican Church in Chorleywood, Herts, England; Gateway Baptist Church in Boswell, New Mexico; Crenshaw Christian Center in Crenshaw, California; and Our Lady of Perpetual Help in Boston, Massachusetts, have all experienced remarkable growth, both numerically as well as in the maturity of their members. Each has an ongoing ministry of signs and wonders.

Power evangelism is not excluded from any culture. We have seen that it can flourish in Western societies with the same results

that occurred in the first century or that are reported from
Africa, South and Central America, and Asia today.

Power versus programme

Over the past seven years, as I have seen the outstanding
response to power evangelism, I have reflected on the reasons
for its success, especially when compared to contemporary
Western evangelistic efforts, most of which I call programmatic
evangelism. A comparison of the two shows significant differences.

Without the aid of charismatic gifts, programmatic evangelism
attempts to reach the minds and hearts of people. Programmatic
evangelism is usually characterised by message-centred com-
municators who present the gospel primarily through rational
arguments. In some cases an appeal to the emotions is also
employed. Usually it is a one-way communication, a prepared
message given by the speaker to passive listeners. There is also
an emphasis on organisation and technique, a search for the
most effective presentation of the gospel, with a tacit assumption
that if people understand the propositions of the gospel they will
decide to become Christians. Of course, there is also the valid
assumption that in its proclamation the gospel has intrinsic
power.

Programmatic evangelism comes in many forms; organised
crusades or revivals, door-to-door saturation campaigns in
which tracts are presented, media campaigns, personal evangelism contacts, friendship evangelism – these are only a few
examples. In each of these the heart of the evangelistic task is a
presentation of several steps needed to enter a relationship with
Christ. These steps are not an adumbration of intellectual arguments for the gospel. They are a simple presentation of the steps
to salvation. An assumption in almost all programmatic evangelism is that reservations in a potential convert are usually intellectual in nature, and thus a high emphasis is placed on answering
theological objections.

By its very nature and assumptions, programmatic evangelism
tends to have as its goal decisions for Christ, not disciples. Many
people who make these decisions do not encounter God's
power, and thus frequently do not move on to a mature

faith. Because there is something inadequate about their conversion experience, later growth for many is retarded.

In programmatic evangelism, Christians witness to everyone they meet, in obedience to the general command of scripture to 'go and make disciples'. In power evangelism, the same command is obeyed, only differently. Each evangelism experience is initiated by the Holy Spirit for a *specific* place, time, person, or group. Instead of indiscriminately spreading the message through a dependence on a preprogrammed message, there is a dependence on the immediate illumination of the Holy Spirit to give pertinent information for each encounter.

In programmatic evangelism, the Christian says, 'In obedience I go. Holy Spirit bless me'. In power evangelism, the Christian says, 'As the Holy Spirit tells me to go, I go'.

In programmatic evangelism, Christians might be fearful as they speak, but they are not unsure about *what* they are going to say before opening their mouths. In power evangelism, Christians are consciously under God's commission and control. They too are fearful as they speak, but they are far more *vulnerable* than in programmatic evangelism because they cannot depend on a prepackaged message. (Fear of losing control is threatening to most Western Christians, something I will comment on further in chapter five.)

In programmatic evangelism there is an attitude that we do something and then God works. In power evangelism, God speaks and then we act.

My contention is not that programmatic evangelism has been wrong. After all, power evangelism employs the heart of programmatic evangelism, a simple presentation of the gospel. Programmatic evangelism has been responsible for bringing millions of people to a personal relationship with Christ. I encourage the practice and development of new kinds of programmatic evangelism. Power envangelism is a catalyst in the programmatic task. My point is that programmatic evangelism is often incomplete, lacking demonstration of the kingdom of God in signs and wonders – but this in no way invalidates the gospel presentation.

C. Peter Wagner, in his book *Frontiers in Missionary Strategy*, introduces a paradigm that describes different goals of evangelism. I have found his model very helpful for understanding how power evangelism and programmatic evangelism help or retard gaining those goals. Dr. Wagner describes three styles based on their goals:

1 *Presence evangelism* is the witness of good works and good deeds (Matthew 5:16). These are not supernatural works such as healing or deliverance from evil spirits; instead, they are acts of mercy, generosity, aid to the poor. The effectiveness of this style of evangelism is measured by how many people are being helped in the name of the Lord. Dr. Wagner calls this 'good evangelism'.

2 *Proclamation evangelism* adds good words to good deeds. The goal here is to help people hear and respond to the gospel (Romans 10:14–15). The emphasis is on helping people make a decision to love Christ.

3 *Persuasion evangelism*, Dr. Wagner says, is the best style of evangelism, because it takes people from the decision phase to the disciple phase. This is the goal of evangelism that Christ calls us to in the great commission passage of Matthew 28:19–20. By 'disciple phase' Wagner means becoming fully *incorporated* into the body of Christ (in a local church). This includes being *taught* the basics of the word of God, *trained* in a Christian way of living that affects every area of a person's life, and *enabling* him or her to do God's works on earth. In sum, the goal of discipleship is that we become, to use C. S. Lewis's term, 'little Christs'[8] – that we take on his character and do his works.

I have discovered that there are many Christians who believe that persuasion evangelism is God's ideal, but they do not know how to lead people beyond the decision stage. They are frustrated in their efforts to make disciples. Most of the programmatic efforts, because of their emphasis on rational decisions, only help people along to the proclamation phase. The methodology and content of programmatic evangelism frequently are insufficient to lead people into the persuasion, or discipleship, stage.

A key to moving from presence to proclamation and into persuasion evangelism is employing *power evangelism*, the demonstration of God's power through signs and wonders. Power evangelism is a catalyst for accelerating the transition through the various phases. In power evangelism key obstacles – adulterous affairs, bitterness, physical ailments, demon possession – are exposed and overcome, striking deeply into the hearts of people. This frees new believers from major obstacles to future spiritual growth. Further, power encounters authenticate conversion experiences in a way that mere intellectual assent does not. This gives new Christians confidence about their conversion, a solid foundation for the rest of their lives.

It is Christ's presence and power that make it possible for people to become mature disciples, to do his works. Without his power we cannot lead people into the discipleship phase.

A revealing question

Shortly after Jesus raised from the dead a man in the city of Nain, John the Baptist sent two of his disciples to ask him, 'Are you the one who was to come, or should we expect someone else?' (Luke 7:19). Jesus did not reply by giving a set of logical proofs in the manner to which we are accustomed. Instead, he validated his ministry from the perspective of a power demonstration of the kingdom of God. Jesus demonstrated that he was the Messiah by the works which he did that fulfilled the Old Testament Messianic prophecies. (In this sense, there is a logic and rationality in his response to John's disciples.) 'Go back and report to John what you have seen and heard: The blind receive sight, the lame walk, those who have leprosy are cured, the deaf hear, the dead are raised, and the good news is preached to the poor.' Jesus was telling the disciples to reassure John by what they had seen and heard – the healing of the sick, the expulsion of evil spirits, the raising of the dead.

These were not sporadic events in Christ's ministry. A close look at scripture reveals that Jesus spent more time healing and casting out demons than preaching. Out of 3,779 verses in the four gospels, 727 (nineteen percent of the total) relate specifically to the healing of physical and mental illness and the resurrection of the dead. Except for discussion about miracles in general, attention devoted to the healing ministry of Jesus is far greater than that devoted to any other aspect of his ministry. John's disciples would have understood from Old Testament prophets like Isaiah that the presence of the Messiah – the embodiment of the kingdom of God – was demonstrated in power encounters.

The early church was effective because it understood evangelism as a testimony that Christ was the fulfilment of messiahship, with powerful demonstrations of the kingdom of God that confirmed his message.

'As the Father has sent me', said Jesus to the disciples after his resurrection, 'I am sending you'. He then breathed the Holy Spirit on them (John 20:21,22). Earlier, after challenging Thomas to believe in him on the basis of his miracles, he had said, 'Anyone who has faith in me will do what I have been doing. He will do even greater things than these . . .' (John 14:11,12). Clearly Jesus envisioned a group of people – his disciples – who would perform not only the same but even greater miracles than he did. The only limitation for receiving this power is lack of faith: '*Anyone* who has faith in me . . .' It was Christ's intention that the kingdom of God be spread in the same way that he spread it – through power evangelism.

Paul's understanding of this perspective accounted for his phenomenal success in Corinth. This understanding came after only a modest response in Athens. In Athens Paul argued eloquently at the Areopagus, with the results that 'a *few* men became followers of Paul and believed' (Acts 17:34). Many Western Christians use Paul's sermon as a model for modern evangelistic efforts, ignoring its meagre results.

In Corinth, the next stop on his apostolic tour, the results were that '*many* people in this city' believed (Acts 18:10). While there are several factors that explain the different responses (particularly the different degrees of receptivity found in the people of each city), Paul himself wrote in 1 Corinthians 2:1 and 5: 'When I came to you brothers, I did not come with eloquence or superior wisdom . . . My message and my preaching were not with wise and persuasive words, but with a demonstration of the Spirit's power, so that your faith might not rest on men's wisdom, but on God's power'. Paul changed his evangelistic methods: in Corinth he combined demonstration with proclamation.

4

THE DIVINE APPOINTMENT

It had been a long day at the office, full of deadlines and meetings that leave editors eager for only one thing: getting home and relaxing with their families. As Kerry Jennings (not his real name) navigated across the freeway system towards his surburban home, he fell into prayer, a habit he had developed to redeem the hours spent in traffic jams. He interceded for his family, co-workers, and friends. He prayed about an article that he was writing. Then he began to ask God to provide opportunities for personal evangelism. Suddenly strange thoughts entered his mind, the accompanying peace indicating the Lord was responding to his prayers. He had acted on these kinds of thoughts before, almost always seeing God work through him.

God told Kerry to stop at a familiar restaurant, look for a certain waitress, and tell her that 'God had something for her.' Further, God said that what he had for the waitress would be revealed when Kerry talked with her. Though apprehensive, Kerry responded to the inkling, steering his car towards the restaurant.

He did so because he sensed that God had arranged a *divine appointment*, an appointed time in which God reveals himself to an individual or group through spiritual gifts or other supernatural phenomena. God arranges these encounters – they are meetings he has ordained to demonstrate his kingdom (Ephesians 2:10).

After being seated in the waitress's section, Kerry began to ponder all the reasons for not delivering the message. While caught up in anxious thoughts, she approached.

Before he could say anything, she cheerfully said, 'You have something for me, don't you'? In response (his resistance now gone), he told her that God had sent him specifically with something, and then two insights regarding her job and a relationship (both areas of trouble for her) were supernaturally revealed to him. Asking God for courage, he told her.

She was stunned. She knew that she was encountering God, because the only way Kerry could know the things he told her was through supernatural means. (In scripture this is called a word of knowledge, see 1 Corinthians 12:8.)

At the end of the conversation they prayed. She cried. Later Kerry learned that she was the daughter of a Christian pastor – now deceased – and that she had turned away from God. Soon after the divine appointment she gave her heart to God.

Divine appointments are an integral part of power evangelism. People who would otherwise resist hearing the gospel are instantly opened to God's word. Sometimes even the most hostile individuals turn to God when a significant need is met.

Serendipity

We should 'always be prepared to give an answer to everyone who asks us to give the reason for the hope that we have' (1 Peter 3:15) – that is, every Christian should always be prepared to proclaim the way of salvation. Yet what I am describing in divine appointments goes beyond the simple explanation of the gospel. While proclamation is an important element of divine appointments, it would be misleading to think of them only as opportunities to explain the way of salvation.

For example, in Luke 19:1–10, we find the story of Jesus coming through the town of Jericho. His encounter with Zacchaeus, the short and unpopular tax-gatherer, is an excellent illustration of a divine appointment. On seeing him, Jesus said, 'Zacchaeus, hurry and come down, for today I must stay at your home'. 'Behold, Lord, half of my possessions I will give to the poor, and if I have defrauded anyone of anything, I will give back four times as much'. What could explain Zacchaeus's remarkable response to such a simple request?

First, Jesus called him by name. There is no indication in scripture that Jesus had any prior knowledge of Zacchaeus. Jesus was doing here what the Holy Spirit enables Christians to do through a word of knowledge, what Kerry Jennings did when he spoke to the waitress. Second, Zacchaeus was hated by the townspeople; as tax-gatherer, he took from the Jews on behalf of the Romans, keeping everything (which was usually a considerable sum of money) that exceeded the Roman requirements. He was a man who probably had few friends. He had a deep need for acceptance and human companionship. Jesus reached out to him and communicated, through a simple request for hospitality, that he loved and accepted him.

Supernatural revelation. The meeting of a deep human need. It is small wonder that Zacchaeus was saved (probably before his feet hit the ground as he jumped from the tree), that all resistance to the gospel was overcome.

There are other lessons to learn from Zacchaeus as well. Many times, God works miracles not so much on account of but in quite different ways from our motivations and actions. Zacchaeus climbed the tree in order to see Christ more clearly, but in doing so was himself more clearly seen by God. In this regard, divine appointments have an air of serendipity about them, a surprising discovery of divine favour.

Illustrations of supernatural, transrational encounters like this in scripture are not exceptional. Another example, perhaps the most striking in the Bible, is the calling of Nathanael in the first chapter of John's gospel.

Too often Western Christians evangelise with a mindset devoid of supernatural presence. We operate in this mindset because we are unaware of the supernatural promptings of the Holy Spirit. Have you ever experienced promptings or thoughts similar to Kerry Jennings, only to dismiss them as the result of a bad cup of coffee? Have you ever experienced flashes of insight when talking to someone, when you knew what their problem or need was before they told you, only to later dismiss it as a lucky intuition? If so, perhaps from now on you should more attentively listen for God's voice, stepping out in faith when you sense his promptings.

The process of conversion

Evangelism is a complex process in which the Holy Spirit works in the hearts and minds of people. Central to the process is communication. Viggo Sogaard offers a model (developed at a 1970 seminar in Bangkok) of the various stages that people frequently go through in coming to full maturity in Christ:

S	*A*	Knows absolutely nothing about the gospel
O		
W	*D*	Had initial exposure to the gospel
I		
N	*G*	Understands some basic characteristics of the gospel
G		
	J	Understands implications of the gospel and way of salvation
R	*M*	
E		
A	*N*	
P		Decision
I	*O*	
N		
G	*R*	
R		New Christian
E	*U*	
F		Mature Christian and lay-reader
I		
N	*X*	Mature and trained leader who is able to teach others
I		
N		
G	*Z*	

In commenting on his model, Sogaard says, 'It should be noted that the model indicates stages, which themselves are processes. Reaping is indicated as a process, and the model has a "conversion point" only for the sake of illustration. The decision point could be at almost any point on the scale, but experience indicates that conversions that are genuine and lasting usually take place after a person has understood the basic characteristics of the gospel. Conversions would therefore usually take place in the area indicated as reaping'.[1]

The goal of the evangelism process is moving people along the scale, from A to Z, not only to a personal conversion experience but also to maturity in Christ.

But this model for understanding the conversion process is

deficient. A second dimension, which takes account of people's attitudes, is also significant in the process.

James F. Engel in his 'Engel Scale' draws from secular research on attitudes in business and politics, showing how attitudes affect the evangelism process.[2]

The Engel Scale integrates knowledge, belief, attitude, intention, and decision in order to help us understand conversion:

−8 Awareness of Supreme Being
−7 Some knowledge of the gospel
−6 Knowledge of fundamentals of gospel
−5 Grasp of personal implications of gospel
−4 Positive attitude toward act of becoming a Christian
−3 Problem recognition and intention to act
−2 Decision to act
−1 Repentance and faith in Christ
    NEW CREATURE
+1 Post decision evaluation
+2 Incorporation into church
+3 Conceptual and behavioural growth

(C. Peter Wagner, observing the incompleteness of the Engel Scale, modified it to include stages of discipleship training and witnessing in word and lifestyle for Christ.)

The Engel Scale is an easy model to understand, and most Christians can quickly place those with whom they are talking on the scale so they can better understand their needs. Once this is done, the gospel message can be adapted to where the person is in thinking and attitude, to his or her needs.

Most Christians, unaware of the Engel Scale, move non-Christians along this scale haphazardly. For example, if we talk with a person that barely has an awareness that there is a Supreme Being (−8 on the Engel Scale) in the same way as someone who grasps the personal implications of the gospel (−5), we will speak a message he cannot understand.

Programmatic evangelism, because it is a planned presentation, inclines Christians towards approaching all non-Christians as though they are at the same place in the conversion process. Of course, poor or no training in personal evangelism also contributes to Christians' incorrectly perceiving non-Christians' attitudes and thinking.

Power evangelism cuts through much resistance that comes from ignorance or negative attitudes. That is, it moves people along the Engel Scale quickly, especially overcoming negative attitudes towards Christianity. By penetrating the inner heart and consciousness, God supernaturally overcomes resistance that through rational means only would take a lifetime – if ever – to work through.

There are two communication dynamics taking place in evangelism: the natural, as described on the Engel Scale; and the supernatural, as seen in power evangelism, in which people are accelerated through the evangelism process.

Power evangelism is not anti-rational. If people are going to be converted, they need to know the essentials of the gospel, that they are sinners in need of God's grace and that grace is experienced through faith in Christ. But simply telling non-believers about Christ does not necessarily mean they will believe in him. Demonstrating the gospel through the gifts of the Spirit supports our message – frequently making persuasive arguments unnecessary – so non-believers can know God's love and power.

An awareness of both dynamics, providing information and power demonstration, most effectively moves people through the Engel Scale.

The difference between power evangelism and programmatic evangelism is analogous to the difference between the impact of a forty-five calibre bullet and buckshot. The forty-five is de-signed to reap havoc on a small target; when accurately aimed – at the place of greatest vulnerability – it is always deadly. In comparison, buckshot is usually less effective, relying more on chance hits. Divine appointments are like the impacts of forty-five calibre bullets: they hit the specific target with penetrating impact.

Several years ago, when the Vineyard Christian Fellowship was meeting in a high school gymnasium, a middle-aged couple out for a walk wandered into the meeting. They had seen parked cars outside the school and were curious about the gathering; they never suspected it was a church meeting.

They knew virtually nothing about Christianity.

Finding a seat in the back of the room (we had begun worship and were singing), within two or three minutes they began to cry.

They did not even know what the meeting was about! They simply liked the music and felt the presence of God. For a reason they did not understand it made them cry. When I asked for anyone who wanted to be saved to come forward, they responded, even though I had not given an evangelistic message.

When asked what they wanted by one of our staff, they answered that they did not know – they had come forward because they could not stop themselves. On hearing a simple presentation of the gospel, they committed themselves to Christ. Of course, with such little knowledge they needed immediate follow-up and instruction.

God's timing and power overcame all reservations. Here we see the wooing power of God operating on a transrational plane. They were drawn not by a message but by a supernatural presence. The message had to be given to complete the process, but without the drawing work of the Holy Spirit, the couple would not have readily accepted it.

Launching points

Scripture is full of illustrations of divine appointments. Probably the most familiar in the life of Christ is found in the fourth chapter of John, the Samaritan woman at Jacob's well.

After asking her for a drink of water, Jesus used water as a launching point to explain spiritual truths. As the dialogue continued it became apparent that the woman had little accurate knowledge about the true nature of God.

Then Jesus said, 'You have had five husbands; and the man you now have is not your husband'. With this statement, he caught her attention. 'Sir, I can see that you are a prophet'. That is, she realised that Christ was a seer, someone who can see the unknown – in this case, her secret sins.

After that she had no resistance to what Christ was saying. The result was that she believed. Through her testimony a revival started in the Samaritan community. 'Come, see a man who told me everything I ever did. Could this be the Christ?'

Through this divine appointment the Samaritan woman moved from some knowledge of God, to repentance, from sin to faith in Christ – all in a matter of minutes!

Several years ago a colleague of mine, Blaine Cook, on a flight from New York to Los Angeles, received a word from God that he was going to lead one of the stewardesses to Christ. An hour into the flight (it is a five-hour trip), Blaine went to the back of the plane and began to talk with her.

During their conversation, the Holy Spirit gave Blaine five specific pieces of information regarding her: she had great fear of never being married; she had just broken a relationship with a man with whom she was living; she had a major conflict with her mother; she was afraid of a physical ailment; and he named specific ailments with which she was afflicted. These thoughts came to him in rapid succession, flashes of intuition that Blaine knew were from God.

He told her what he knew.

She immediately began to cry and asked him how he knew these things. 'I know someone', he replied, 'who will never leave you or forsake you, and will heal you of your sicknesses'. He prayed over her. She was physically healed. She then prayed to become a Christian.

A year later he was about to catch a plane back to New York, and God told him that he would see the stewardess again. When he boarded the plane, there she was. She told him how she had joined a church in Manhattan, had not suffered any symptoms from her illnesses since he prayed over her, and was engaged to marry a Christian. As was true for the Samaritan woman, the stewardess's resistance was supernaturally overcome – the divine appointment motivated her to listen to the claims of the gospel and believe.

Pathways to God

In Acts 8:26–40 we read of another divine appointment involving one of the disciples. Philip was told by an angel to go south of Jerusalem to Gaza. He was then directed to go up to the chariot of an Ethiopian eunuch, a court official of the queen of the Ethiopians. (There is a high probability that to obey the Lord took great courage on Philip's part, for it is likely that as a high official the eunuch would have been heavily guarded. To approach such a man without permission could have meant death.)

At the time the Ethiopian eunuch was reading from Isaiah

53:7–8. On the Engel Scale, the eunuch was at the decision point (−2); he only needed knowledge about what to believe. In God's providence, Philip was sent to explain the next step to him. In order for this to happen, Philip had to be listening to God and obedient to his word.

After the Ethiopian eunuch's baptism, Philip was supernaturally transported away. To this day the eunuch is honoured as the founder of the Ethiopian church.

The harvest was ripe, but a willing worker was needed.

Frequently God arranges divine appointments for people with significant personal problems. We should not be surprised at this. At the beginning of his ministry, at the temple in Nazareth, Jesus proclaimed that his mission was to 'preach good news to the poor . . . freedom for the prisoners and recovery of sight for the blind, to release the oppressed, to proclaim the year of the Lord's favour' (Luke 4:18–19).

Difficult or dire human predicaments are pathways to bring people to salvation. By being more sensitive to the needs of those around us we frequently find situations in which we too can 'proclaim the year of the Lord's favour'.

The story of Jairus's daughter, found in Mark 5, is an excellent example of this. Jairus, a synagogue ruler, had a need: his little daughter was dying. While on the way to heal Jairus's daughter, Jesus was delayed when a woman who had been bleeding for twelve years touched him. She was healed.

During this delay, news came that Jairus's daughter had died. In response to the message, Jesus told Jairus, 'Don't be afraid; just believe'. On entering the home where the daughter lay, Jesus told those who were mourning that the child was only asleep.

They laughed at him, because they thought that he was ignorant of the facts. In first-century, Middle-Eastern society, everyone knew about life and death. The daily slaughter of animals for food or ritual observance familiarised them with death in a way to which most modern people are not accustomed. Infant mortality was very high. Because of this, it was especially difficult for them to see Jairus's daughter as anything but dead.

As Jews their understanding about the resurrection of the dead was probably similar to Christ's: they expected a time, in the Age to Come, when the dead would rise. What they did not expect was that Jesus incarnated the resurrection. But the girl's death gave Christ an opportunity to demonstrate the kingdom of God, and in so doing the witnesses learned more about his true nature.

Many times we struggle with the same limitations as the Jews, the same inability to understand when God tells us to do something out of the ordinary – for example to describe the personal sin of a stranger, as Blaine Cook did with the stewardess. Most Christians miss out on exciting and powerful experiences in their lives, either because they are not listening to God or because of their inattentiveness God is silent.

After putting the sceptics out of the house, Jesus took the parents and Peter, James, and John into the room with the girl. He then said, 'Little girl, I say to you, get up!' The response of those present was astonishment; Jesus instructed them not to tell anyone about what had happened. While not explicitly in the text, we may infer that Jairus and his household put their faith in Christ that day.

In October 1984 I witnessed a similar conversion in London. An Orthodox priest and his sister, a nun, brought their father and three siblings to a conference at which I was speaking. Their father was suffering from diabetes and blindness.

During one of the meetings God told me that someone in the audience was blind, the cause of the blindness being diabetes. In this instance I had received a mental picture of the man's eye with the word diabetes coming to mind. (Sometimes I receive pain in parts of my body that parallels the ailments of people whom God wants to heal. At other times I have a flash of intuition about someone. Over the years I have learned to recognise when these insights are from God and when they are a result of my imagination – or indigestion.)

I announced this to the gathering, along with instruction that this person come forward to be healed by Jesus. (It was a large crowd; I had no prior knowledge of this man.)

The father was healed. He received sight! As a result the other five members of the family encountered God's power. After the meetings, their testimony was, 'Now we know God in a way we never knew him before'.

My point is not that they became Christians (they already had faith in Christ), but that their faith took on a new meaning and depth of commitment. This illustrates how we move people along the Engel Scale even after their conversion, in this instance at the point of conceptual and behavioural growth (+3).

Whole households

The goal of evangelism is not only the creation of individual disciples of Jesus, it also includes building bodies of people, the body of Christ. We have been created by God for fellowship. Right relationships are a part of God's plan for our lives. Because of this corporate or social dimension, we should not be surprised that God frequently brings clusters of people to his kingdom at one time.

Many times we are too focused on individuals, forgetting that when one member of a family or social grouping is affected it can result in a whole family or town being won.

This was a common occurrence in the early church.

As was true of the Philippian jailer and his household in Acts chapter 16, we read in John's gospel of a royal official from Capernaum whose whole household was saved through power evangelism. He came seeking Jesus, asking him to heal his son. After rebuking the official for needing to 'see miraculous signs and wonders' in order to believe, Jesus healed his son. What is unique about this miracle is that Jesus did not lay hands on the boy and pray over him. He simply declared the miracle done and told the official to go home. His son was healed. In response to the supernatural meeting of the official's need, 'he and all his household believed'.

Blaine Cook tells of a similar experience that he had in 1984 at a Baptist Church in a midwestern American city. The pastor of this church of 250 people had invited him to speak about healing. Many who attended were hostile to his message.

During one of his talks Blaine said that he had a word of knowledge – he received a mental picture – regarding healing for a woman with an arthritic elbow. A member of the congregation, the daughter of a coal miner, was prayed for and healed.

The next day this woman brought her daughter to be prayed over. The girl was born hydrocephalitic – she suffered from fourteen neurological conditions, including spina bifida. She was healed instantly of a wandering eye, bedwetting, and an open spine.

Her grandfather, an elder in the church who until then had refused to come to the meetings, came the following day. He was closed to God acting here and now in the way that Blaine taught, being particularly antagonistic towards the charismatic gifts. Though at first very hostile to Blaine's teaching, he relented and came because of what had happened to his daughter and grand-daughter. He could not deny the physical changes. During the meeting he too was healed, and for the first time put his full trust in Christ.

Before the meetings ended, most of the church was affected by what happened to the family, with many *elders* growing in their understanding of the kingdom of God and acceptance of the supernatural. In a few cases, elders admitted that they had been living more of a cultural Christianity than a true heartfelt faith. In the case of 'spiritual leaders' in need of true, heartfelt conversion (a crossing of the Engel Scale's −1 point, repentance and faith in Christ), usually only supernatural encounters break through barriers of pride, religious hypocrisy, and spiritual blindness.

Our part first

In divine appointments and the meeting of human needs the burden of responsibility for mediating the kingdom of God rests on Christians. Through obedient and teachable individuals God is able to perform signs and wonders, thus moving people along the Engel Scale more quickly than normally happens in programmatic evangelism.

Not only individuals and families, but whole towns are converted when God's power is released on hearts and minds.

The villages of Lydda and Sharon were converted when Aeneas, a paralytic who had been bedridden for eight years, was instantly healed by Peter. As was true of Jesus, Peter used a simple and direct style in praying over Aeneas: 'Jesus Christ heals you. Get up and take up your mat' (Acts 9:34). Unlike Jesus, Peter did not heal in his own authority. Christ was the healer.

The evangelistic task was made easy for Peter, because of

Aeneas's healing. Most people respond to acts of mercy and demonstrations of spiritual power.

There is an attitude which is required to keep divine appointments, the one that permeated Jesus' and Peter's lives and which asks how can God use me? Our part, as Jesus taught the Pharisees when they asked him about the greatest commandment, is to 'love the Lord your God with all your heart and with all your soul and with all your mind' (Matthew 22:37). Divine appointments are occasions in which God chooses to do his works through our obedience, faith, hope, and love. They are *his* works, acts to which we add nothing.

This is a difficult attitude for Western Christians to attain, because we are trained to think that only the material is real, and that the supernatural is fantasy. The reasons why this is so, and how to overcome them, are the topics of the next chapter.

5

SIGNS AND WONDERS AND WORLDVIEWS

Shortly after World War II, sociologists went to the Far East to investigate Asians' attitudes and thinking processes, to see how their thinking differed from the West's. They interviewed several thousand people, receiving surprising responses to questions based on logic syllogisms – questions based on rational processes. A typical question was 'Cotton doesn't grow in cold-weather countries. England is a cold-weather country. Does cotton grow in England?' The majority of the Asians who answered the question said that they were not qualified to answer, because 'I haven't been to England'.

In Western nations, most third-grade children would have responded, 'No. Cotton cannot grow in England. It is too cold'. From earliest childhood, Western people are trained in deductive reasoning – based on rules of logic, we draw conclusions that guide our lives. The presuppositions of our culture encourage us to think this way. The assumptions of most Eastern, African, and South American cultures do not – their cultures have more of an experiential base. The exception to this is found among formally educated people. (I am not implying that our culture is superior to Asians, only that it is different.)

The sociologists in Asia encountered cultures in conflict – their own with the Asians'. Under the surface of these cultures there are different ways of understanding how the world works. The Asians' worldview had heavy doses of animism – the belief that material objects possess a soul or spirit – thus they did not practise deductive reasoning. They believed that spirits determine events. Spirits, they thought, are fickle, unpredictable. Asians still could not predict its growth, even if the climatic conditions are right for growing cotton. The sociologists' world-view, on the other hand, was influenced by Western materialism and rationalism – their world was closed to supernatural intervention, so they relied on scientific observation to draw their conclusions.

Author James Sire defines a worldview as 'a set of presuppositions (or assumptions) that we hold (consciously or subconsciously) about the basic makeup of our world'.[1] Most of us are not conscious of our worldview. We do not learn it so much as absorb it from our surrounding culture. It is passed on from generation to generation with minimal change, the assumptions rarely being reviewed or revised. We assume that the way we understand life is how everybody does (or should) and that our understanding of the world is reality.

Every culture has presuppositions, some conscious and many unconscious. We acquire paradigms – thinking patterns with which we evaluate our experiences – from parents, the media, art, education, and so on. Our worldview is like a lens – it colours, clarifies, classifies, warps, or excludes the world. It is, in Charles Kraft's words, our 'control box' of reality.[2]

Cultural cohesiveness

Dr. Kraft, in his book, *Christianity in Culture*, gives a more comprehensive definition of a worldview:

> Cultures pattern perceptions of reality into conceptualizations of what reality can or should be, what is to be regarded as actual, probable, possible, and impossible . . . The worldview is the central systematization of conceptions of reality to which the members of the culture assent (largely unconsciously) and from which stems their value system. The worldview lies at the very heart of the culture, touching, interfacing with, and strongly influencing every aspect of culture.[3]

Worldviews are necessary in the formation and maintenance of cultures. As Christians, our goal is not to shed entirely the worldview of whatever culture we might live in. Instead, our goal is to become self-conscious of our worldview, altering our worldview where it endorses values that are contrary to Christianity.

Dr. Kraft points out these four functions of a worldview:

1 A worldview provides an *explanation* of how and why things are as they are, and how and why they continue or change. These explanations are passed from generation to generation through folklore, myth, stories. They also give the culture structure, a subconscious legitimacy in the minds of the people.

2 A worldview serves as a basis for *evaluation*, judging and validating experience. It is a yardstick with which people measure events and circumstances in the culture, providing criteria of acceptability.

For example, we find in the United States a worldview in which personal influence and material affluence are very important to life. This results in equating success with visible influence and material affluence. This worldview affects American Christians too. They might reject conspicuous material consumption and status seeking lifestyles, but frequently their way of judging 'successful' churches nevertheless reflects the general culture's worldview: large congregations with big budgets are successful. When the Vineyard Christian Fellowship was a small, struggling – and controversial – church, I was shunned by many former colleagues and friends. Then we began to draw large numbers of people. Suddenly the Vineyard Christian Fellowship became a legitimate institution, acceptable in their eyes even though our so-called 'controversial teachings' and practices had not changed. We had met their criteria for success: a large and growing membership and budget.

3 A worldview provides *psychological reinforcement* for a society's way of life. It creates a 'we–they' dynamic: through a common worldview people identify with their society as opposed to all other societies. By accepting and living out the culture's worldview, one senses belonging to the larger group. This provides a sense of safety from fear of foreign values that might disrupt family, occupation, religion. It also creates an environment in which relationships can grow – people are fairly confident that their neighbours see the world as they do, so they freely interact. A sense of community and membership in the clan, tribe, or nation is a byproduct of this psychological reinforcement. As the worldview is continually reinforced, the community is strengthened.

4 A worldview serves an *integrating* function for new informa-

tion, values, philosophies, experiences. Not all new experiences that violate a culture's worldview are rejected outright. Some alter the culture, eventually creating a change in worldview. In this respect, worldviews are always evolving. Worldviews that resist evolution isolate their people from the rest of the world, making their cultures difficult to penetrate. Islamic cultures are excellent examples of this; they are without question the most resistant cultures to new ideas and values, including the gospel. Christian missionaries find Islamic cultures very difficult to penetrate.

Premodern, less technological worldviews – such as those found among American Indians or African tribal peoples – create highly penetrable and fragile cultures. This is especially true when they encounter modern, technological cultures. The invaders have a shattering impact, leaving serious social problems in their wake, as the history of the American Indian all too tragically illustrates.

Secularised Western worldviews create societies that are highly penetrable but resistant to change. Non-Western worldviews (e.g. those found in Hindu, Islamic, or Communist societies) easily penetrate Western culture. But soon the alien worldviews are blunted, absorbed, digested, transformed – usually losing their vitality and ability to profoundly influence the society. This absorbing, digesting, blunting process also affects Christianity, tacitly secularising the faith.[4]

Western worldview

Harry Blamires, in his book, *The Christian Mind*, describes the dominant element of the modern Western worldview as secularism. 'To think secularly', he writes, 'is to think within a frame of reference bounded by the limits of our life on earth: it is to keep one's calculations rooted in this-worldly criteria'. The assumption of secular minds is that we live in a universe closed off from divine intervention, in which truth is arrived at through empirical means and rational thought.

Inherent in the modern Western worldview is a desire to control everything – people, things, events, even future events. The fifteenth-century Renaissance and later Reformation created an appetite in men and women to know more about nature. In swinging away from the medieval resignation of accepting all experiences as God's will, Western society eventually swung to the other extreme during the Enlightenment, making man the measure of all things. By the nineteenth century, materialism was entrenched in the Western worldview.

Materialism assumes that nothing exists except matter and its movements and modifications. For a materialist, only what can be seen, tested, and proved is real. The scientific method is elevated to Holy Writ. Working from this presupposition, Western people have learned to observe regularities and patterns in the material world, and develop a series of laws and principles for almost all areas of life: medicine, physics, philosophy, psychology, economics, and so on. These explanations are thought of as consistent, stable, and dependable.

Christians cannot be philosophical materialists and retain a Christian worldview. Nevertheless, we are influenced by materialism. It warps our thinking, softening convictions about the supernatural world of angels and demons, heaven and hell, Christ and antichrist. We often live as though the material world is more real than the spiritual, as though material cause-and-effect explains all of what happens to us.

Rationalism seeks a rational explanation for all experience, making reason the chief guide in all matters of life. Because angels, demons, God, and spiritual gifts like tongues or prophecy cannot be scientifically measured, secularists employ rationalism to explain away the supernatural. The root problem for rejecting the supernatural is not that secularists believe in cause and effect, though; it is because they exclude from reality all phenomena that cannot be measured scientifically.

Twentieth-century rationalism is not necessarily an attempt to be rigorously rational. We must differentiate twentieth-century rationalism from the rationalism of the Enlightenment in the eighteenth century. During the Enlightenment many materialists thought it was possible to rationally analyse all experience, arriving at objective truth, even in areas like morality. Modern rationalists no longer believe this is possible. In fact, there are many rational inconsistencies in the way secularists think. For example, while believing in a closed material universe that may be understood only by scientific inquiry, at the same time they hold relativistic assumptions about religion and morality. Believing that 'whatever you believe is okay for you' assumes a plurality of moral systems. In this regard most secularised people hold an internally inconsistent worldview.

This accounts for the current growth in many Western societies of pseudo-eastern religions like EST and Transcendental Meditation. On the surface this seems to contradict what one would expect from a materialistic worldview. In fact, irrational religion naturally flows from the inconsistencies inherent in rationalism. Most modern secularists are not rigorously rational – they frequently acknowledge there is an irrational spiritual or moral world that can only be known through personal experience.

In the final analysis, materialism and rationalism are big lies, incapable of providing plausible explanations for meaning in life. The secular worldview fails to satisfy people's need to understand the universe, so they look for that meaning elsewhere, even in irrational philosophies and religions.

The Eastern religions' 'faith', unlike Christian faith, is relativistic, subjective, and irrational – a blind leap into the supernatural. The experiences of Christian signs and wonders are *transrational*, but they serve a rational purpose: to authenticate the gospel. The gospel is opposed to the pluralistic lie that says all religious experience is equally valid. Signs and wonders validate Christ's lordship over every area of our lives, a relationship that can be described and understood.

Christian worldview

'To think christianly', writes Harry Blamires, a former student of C. S. Lewis, 'is to accept all things with the mind as related, directly or indirectly, to man's eternal destiny as the redeemed and chosen child of God'.[5] For Blamires, thinking christianly is equated with holding a Christian worldview. In his book, *The Christian Mind*, Blamires mentions several elements in a Christian worldview:

1 'A prime mark of the Christian mind is that *it cultivates the eternal perspective* . . . It is supernaturally orientated, and brings to bear upon earthly considerations the fact of Heaven and the fact of Hell.'[6] This presupposition means that Christians believe in an open universe, a world in which God freely speaks and acts.

This sets Christians in direct conflict with Western materialists, who live on the basis that this world is all there is to life.

2 'The Christian mind has an *acute and sensitive awareness of the power and spread of evil upon the human race*'.[7] Evil – the world, the flesh, and the Devil – is constantly assaulting God's people. This awareness of evil means that Christians see themselves as members of an army, living in an alien land, locked in combat with Satan. There really is sin. There are evil spirits lurking about in the world. This awareness of evil also motivates Christians to rely on the Holy Spirit to overcome the Evil One.

3 'The *conception of truth* proper to the Christian mind is determined by the supernatural orientation of the Christian mind . . . truth is supernaturally grounded: it is not manufactured within nature'.[8] In this regard, all experience is judged by God's revelation, whereas for the secularist truth is judged by the subjective self. For Christians, then, there is objective truth – rational propositions about God, the creation and morality that can be known and which are eternal. We believe in transcendent moral standards to which we can submit every aspect of our thinking.

Other elements that Blamires mentions are Christians' acceptance of God's authority and a high sense of the value of human persons.

At every point, the Christian worldview is in conflict with the secular mind. Yet many Western Christians are unaware of the conflict, because in large part they have been secularised. A way of understanding how far many Christians' thinking is from God's ideals is by comparing the twentieth-century evangelical church with the first century church. Jack Rogers, in his book *Confessions of a Conservative Evangelical*, gives these general characteristics of a culture informed by a worldview that sees all human activity as directly or indirectly related to God:

1 *Scripture values the contemplative life*. This is a result of holding a supernatural worldview. Because a biblical worldview rejects materialism, therefore meditation on eternal truths, God's word, is of high value. An example of this is Psalm 77, where the psalmist 'remembered [his] songs in the night' and '[his] heart mused and [his] spirit enquired' of God (verse 6). Modern, technological society, so concerned with time ('time is money'),

has little patience for activity that has no apparent material benefit, that is rooted outside of time. (Perhaps this is one reason most Western Christians struggle with personal prayer.)

2 *Scripture is poetic*. This value comes from the Christian's understanding of revelation being rooted in the supernatural, testifying to a reality beyond the temporal order. Intrinsic to this transcendent reality is beauty. So anything worth saying is worth saying beautifully. For example, Psalm 1 is a poetic picture of a righteous man. Relativism places a higher value on pragmatism, which is more concerned with 'Does it work' than 'Is it beautiful'.

3 *The Bible employs vivid picture language*. Because God actually speaks and affects the material world, descriptions of how he works convey eternal truth. A first-century semitic person did not argue from a premise to a conclusion – he was not controlled by rationalism. Instead, he painted a word picture, employing concrete situations, relationships, and places to make his point. There was a mistrust (or inability to comprehend) theological truths through abstract reasoning, which is the opposite of Western culture today.

Instead, the Bible frequently uses symbolic language. Concrete objects can symbolise theological truths. Scripture is loaded with metaphors, similes, and other figures of speech. Western Christians, on the other hand, tend to make literal what is frequently supposed to be taken as figurative.

4 *Scripture accepts paradox easily*. For example, Western Christians have always found it difficult to accept the paradoxical truths of God's sovereignty and man's freedom. They are preoccupied with logical consistency, a concern that first-century Christians did not have. Yet both doctrines are found in scripture, and they were not a topic of concern in the early church. Their worldview allowed for apparent contradiction when touching on the mysteries of God. The Western church, more concerned with theological precision, has produced thousands of books trying to reconcile the two.

5 *Religion is a way of life*. Relativism levels all competing belief systems in a society, making it impossible to develop conventions and traditions. Historian Christopher Lasch and sociologist Peter Berger have observed that modern Western societies lack consistent patterns of community, family life, even religion.

Lacking transcendent moral standards, Western culture tends to be protean, changing its form with every new fad.

Christianity, rooted in God's revelation and a highly developed sense of membership in the body of Christ, sees Christian truth touching every area of a person's life. Because God's revelation never changes and touches every area of life, Christians can with confidence build distinctly Christian social environments and lifestyles.

But Western Christians have found it difficult to build distinctively Christian lifestyles. Distilling Christian teaching down to a set of creeds and a code of ethics, they are usually more concerned with personal conduct and assent to doctrine than with Christian lifestyle. They hold more of a Christian ethic or practice, not a way of life. But Christianity is much more than a list of beliefs to which we assent. Western Christians are concerned with following the 'Christian rules'; early Christians lived in Christian communities in which every aspect of life – work, play, family, relationships – reflected a Christian way of doing things.

Twentieth-century Islam is comprehensive in its application of religious teaching to daily life. Law, economics, education, and almost every area of culture reflect Islamic teaching in nations like Iran and Saudi Arabia. In this respect, modern Islam more closely reflects the way and extent in which Christian values affected a way of life among first-century Christians than does Western Christianity today.[9]

This list could be greatly expanded. Each of the above characteristics challenges a fundamental component of the Western worldview. The Christian's challenge is to alter his worldview where it works against these biblical characteristics. If we do not alter our worldview, we will misunderstand scripture, missing what God is teaching about how he works in the world.

The excluded middle

Everyone has cultural blindspots, those areas of life from which we exclude God. They are areas that Satan loves to take advantage of, exploiting our inability to see or understand key aspects of the kingdom of God.

Animism, as I wrote above, is the belief that all objects in the material world are inhabited by souls or spirits. This kind of worldview has a tremendous impact on peoples' ability to reason abstractly. It affects their understanding of cause and effect, in many instances causing them great harm. For example, modern medicine, built on the Western scientific assumption of material cause and effect, has assumed smallpox has a physical cause. Through scientific research, modern doctors developed a smallpox vaccine. They have largely eradicated smallpox in societies that receive smallpox vaccinations. But in many animist cultures where they understand the cause of all smallpox to be evil spirits, smallpox vaccination has not been accepted, resulting in untold death and misery.

Western worldviews have the opposite problem. Because secularists believe in a closed universe of material cause and effect, they cannot accept supernatural intervention. Christians who are influenced by this aspect of Western worldview find healing, especially when the cause for illness is an evil spirit, difficult to understand or accept.

Dr. Paul Hiebert, a professor in the Fuller Seminary School of World Missions, had this blindspot when he first went on the mission field:

> John's disciples ask, 'Are you he, the one who was to come, or should we expect someone else?' (Luke 7:20). Jesus answered not with logical proofs, but by a demonstration of power in the curing of the sick and casting out of evil spirits. So much is clear. Yet when I read the passage as a missionary in India, and sought to apply it to missions in our day, I had a strange uneasiness. As a Westerner, I was used to presenting Christ on the basis of rational arguments, not by evidences of his power in the lives of people who were sick, possessed, and destitute. In particular, *the confrontation with spirits that appeared so natural a part of Christ's ministry belonged in my mind to a separate world of the miraculous – far from ordinary everyday experience* [emphasis mine].

Dr. Hiebert's 'strange uneasiness' was soon tested by a smallpox plague in the village:

> Doctors trained with Western medicine had tried to halt the smallpox but had not succeeded. The village elders finally sent for a diviner who told them that Maisamma, the

Goddess of Smallpox, was angry at the village. To satisfy her and stop the plague, the villagers would have to perform a water buffalo sacrifice. Their elders had to collect money to buy the water buffalo. The Christians refused to give any money. The elders got angry and forbade them to draw water from the wells and made the merchants refuse to sell them food. One of the elders of the Church in that village had come to get me [Dr. Hiebert] at the mission station to pray for the healing of one of the Christian girls who was sick with smallpox. As I knelt, my mind was in turmoil. I had learned to pray as a child, studied prayer in seminary, preached it as a pastor. But now I was to pray for a sick child as all the village watched to see if the Christian God could heal.

He then posed the question: 'Why my uneasiness both with reading the scripture and in the Indian village? Was the problem, at least in part, due to my own worldview – to the assumptions I as a Westerner made about the nature of reality and the way I viewed the world?' He then answered his own question:

People in the Indian villages have many diseases, curses of barrenness on women, bad tempers, bad luck, being possessed by spirits, and black magic practices. The Indian villages have traditional ways of dealing with diseases:

1 *Serious life threatening cases:* With these cases they take the person to a *sadhu* – a 'saint'. This is a person of the gods who claims to heal by prayer. Because god knows everything they ask no questions. Because they are spiritual they charge no fees. But one is expected to give if a cure comes about.

2 *Supernatural cases:* With these cases they go to a *Mantrakar* – a 'magician'. This one cures by knowledge and control of supernatural forces and spirits, believed to be here on earth. They work with chants and visual symbols to control the forces and spirits. They ask no questions, receive no fees.

3 *Medicine:* Some people would go to doctors who cure by means of scientific knowledge based on medicine. They ask no questions but diagnose by feeling wrists, stomachs,

etc. They charge high fees and give a guarantee that one only pays if the patient is healed.

4 *Quacks:* These people heal with folk remedies. They ask questions, charge low fees, give no guarantees. The people being treated have to pay before receiving treatment. (At the beginning, Western doctors were often equated with quacks.)

When a person became a Christian, he substituted the missionary for the saint! Christ replaced Krishna or Siva as the healer of their spiritual diseases. For the illnesses they had, they went to Western doctors or village quacks. But what about the plagues that the magician cured? What about spirit possession, or curses, or witchcraft, or black magic? What was the Christian answer to these?

Because of the Western culture's assumptions, the only conclusion one had was 'They do not exist'. But to the people who really experienced these phenomena, there had to be an answer. So even the Christians turned to the magician for cures.[10]

Upon further reflection of his missionary experience, Dr. Hiebert uncovered a blindspot in his worldview. To describe his blindspot, he developed a three-tiered model of his Western worldview. The chart (see p 86, top) summarises his thinking.

The key tier on this chart is the 'excluded middle'. By dividing the universe into two totally separate worlds, Dr. Hiebert (and many Westerners, including Christians) excluded supernatural intervention in the material universe. Another way in which the chart could be drawn, one which highlights the sharp separation between the natural and supernatural, is to draw a thick, impenetrable line between the upper and lower tiers (see p 86, bottom).

TRANSCENDENT WORLD BEYOND OURS: *includes* – hells, heavens, other times i.e. eternity – high god (African); Vishnu, Siva (Hindu) – cosmic forces; karma – Jehovah, angels, demons, spirits of worlds	RELIGION faith sacred miracles other-worldly problems
SUPERNATURAL FORCES ON THIS EARTH: *includes* – spirits, ghosts, ancestors, demons – earthly gods and goddesses who live within trees, rivers, hills, villages – supernatural forces: mana, planetary influences, evil eyes, power of magic, sorcery, witchcraft – Holy Spirit, angels, demons, *Signs and Wonders*, gifts of the Spirit	EXCLUDED MIDDLE by Westerners

EMPIRICAL WORLD OF OUR SENSES:
includes
– folk sciences to explain how things occur
– explanations based on empirical observations
  ●person shoots an arrow into a deer – he attributes
  death to arrow
  ●one cooks a meal – attributes 'cooked meal' to fire
  under pot
– theories about natural world –
  ●how to build a house; plant crops; sail canoe
– theories about human relationships –
  ●how to raise children; treat spouse, etc.
	SCIENCE
	sight &
	experience
	natural order
	secular
	this-worldly
	problems

TRANSCENDENT WORLD BEYOND OURS: *includes* – hells, heavens, other times i.e. eternity – high god (African); Vishnu, Siva (Hindu) – cosmic forces; karma – Jehovah, angels, demons, spirits of worlds	RELIGION faith sacred miracles other-worldly problems

EMPIRICAL WORLD OF OUR SENSES:
includes
– folk sciences to explain how things occur
– explanations based on empirical observations
  ●person shoots an arrow into a deer – he attributes
  death to arrow
  ●one cooks a meal – attributes 'cooked meal' to fire
  under pot
– theories about natural world –
  ●how to build a house; plant crops; sail canoe
– theories about human relationships –
  ●how to raise children; treat spouse, etc.
	SCIENCE
	sight &
	experience
	natural order
	secular
	this-worldly
	problems

Animism and most eastern religions obliterate the barrier between the transcendent and empirical tiers. This confuses the spiritual and material worlds, resulting in frequently ascribing spiritual causes to physical problems that have physical roots. Using the adapted Hiebert chart, the animist's world looks like this:

TRANSCENDENT WORLD BEYOND OURS: *includes* – hells, heavens, other times i.e. eternity – high god (African); Vishnu, Siva (Hindu) – cosmic forces; karma – Jehovah, angels, demons, spirits of worlds	**RELIGION** faith sacred miracles other-worldly problems

EMPIRICAL WORLD OF OUR SENSES:
 includes
 – folk sciences to explain how things occur
 – explanations based on empirical observations
   ●person shoots an arrow into a deer – he attributes
    death to arrow
   ●one cooks a meal – attributes 'cooked meal' to fire
    under pot
 – theories about natural world –
   ●how to build a house; plant crops; sail canoe
 – theories about human relationships –
   ●how to raise children; treat spouse, etc.
	SCIENCE
	 sight &
	 experience
	 natural order
	 secular
	 this-worldly
	 problems

Of course, the world does not divide neatly into two groups – primitive animists and rationalistic materialists. There are many variations between these two extremes. For example, people who do not believe there is a transcendent reality – modern atheists, for example – would deny there is an upper tier. Most communists fall in this category.

The biblical worldview opens but does not obliterate the barrier between the lower and upper tiers. Completely removing the barrier leads to pantheism (equating God with the creation). The Christian worldview makes room for mystery in the relationship between the spiritual and material worlds. For example, the Christian worldview sees some illness as caused directly by demons and other illness having physical causes. Instead of being forced to the extremes of empiricism or animism, Christians see the *possibility though not the necessity* for supernatural intervention in all earthly experience. Again adapting the Hiebert model, the Christian worldview would look like this:

TRANSCENDENT WORLD BEYOND OURS: *includes* – hells, heavens, other times i.e. eternity – high god (African); Vishnu, Siva (Hindu) – cosmic forces; karma – Jehovah, angels, demons, spirits of worlds	RELIGION faith sacred miracles other-worldly problems

EMPIRICAL WORLD OF OUR SENSES:
includes
– folk sciences to explain how things occur
– explanations based on empirical observations
  ●person shoots an arrow into a deer – he attributes
    death to arrow
  ●one cooks a meal – attributes 'cooked meal' to fire
    under pot
– theories about natural world –
  ●how to build a house; plant crops; sail canoe
– theories about human relationships –
  ●how to raise children; treat spouse, etc.
	SCIENCE
	sight &
	experience
	natural order
	secular
	this-worldly
	problems

Many Christians unconsciously consign the supernatural to an impenetrable upper tier (except for the resurrection, early church miracles, and transcendent moral standards), excluding God's power from their theology and practice. Resisting that which they cannot fully control or always understand, they miss out on doing Christ's works today.

Learning to see

Worldviews exert a powerful influence in the minds of people. Probably their greatest source of power is that few people are conscious of their worldviews. But human beings are not robots, programmed by the hand of culture. A group's worldview does not completely determine the perceptions of its individual members or subgroupings at all times. We interact with contrary worldviews as there is opportunity, through travel, reading, new relationships, or even contact with the many immigrant subgroupings within society.

Many evangelicals sincerely think that only scripture study forms their thinking on such issues as healing or power evangelism. They are unaware of how powerful the influences of a Western, materialistic worldview are and how that worldview affects their perception of the supernatural in scripture. Dr.

Hiebert described this effect as a 'strange uneasiness' when asked to pray for the sick girl.

Western Christians must undergo a paradigm (or perception) shift to become involved in a signs and wonders ministry. This is a shift towards a worldview that makes room for God's miraculous intervention. It is not that we allow God's intervention: he does not need our permission. The shift is that we begin to *see* his miraculous works and *allow* them to affect our lives.

Our ability to see and understand different phenomena is learned. Sometimes, because we have a different view of something or because we have not learned what to look for, we cannot see what is obvious to others. An analogy can be drawn from viewing the drawing below:

What do you see? A young lady or an old hag? Some see a young lady, then, looking at the picture differently, an old hag. Others only see one or the other, until someone shows them how to see the image differently. The lines of the drawing do not shift, the perception of the observer does. This, on a small scale, is analogous to a worldview change, a paradigm shift.

There is a process involved in learning to see the picture differently. It is difficult to see that which you have not seen before. When first seeing it, you do not comprehend it. Seeing in this respect is learned over a period of time, most people being unaware of the process.

So we do not see or notice everything we look at. We have selective perception. In the New Testament, dreams and visions are one of the means of communication that God uses in speaking to his people. They are even described as a normal part of the Christian life. Peter, quoting from Joel's prophecy, promised that the day had arrived when 'your young men will see visions, your old men will dream dreams' (Acts 2:17). Yet how often do Western evangelicals today report dreams and visions? Is it because God is not revealing himself in this fashion or because a blindspot in our worldview prevents us from seeing what God is doing?

In many African tribal societies, dreams and visions are readily acknowledged and talked about among the people. Influenced by animism, they interpret such experiences from a spiritual, not psychological, perspective. When these people become Christians, they continue to attach spiritual significance to their dreams, only now seeing them coming from Jesus. (I am not implying here that all dreams are from Jesus, only that some may be and that these phenomena are common in scripture.)

Many third-world missionaries on furlough attend my course on signs and wonders at Fuller Seminary. After I lecture on worldview, they usually comment to me on their inability to discuss supernatural phenomena when they are in the United States. Magic, sorcery, witchcraft – frequently seen on the mission field – are viewed by many of the missionaries' American brothers and sisters as fantastic superstition, manifestations of 'natives'' ignorance. If the missionaries describe these spiritual phenomena as though real, they risk their credibility with financial supporters. So most missionaries remain silent.

Could it be that many Western evangelicals have subconsciously developed a theology that excludes the possibility of supernaturally inspired dreams and visions, harmonising 'Christian doctrine' with Western rationalism? This is not to question motives, only to note that worldview inhibits many evangelicals from seeing or accepting miracles.

I went through a process of learning to see the kingdom of God, of adjusting my worldview, as I began a signs and wonders ministry. Jesus taught the disciples about spiritual eyesight in response to their questions concerning the parable of the sower and the seeds in Matthew 13:11–16:

The knowledge of the secrets of the kingdom of heaven has been given to you, but not to them . . . This is why I speak to them in parables:
'Though seeing, they do not see; though hearing, they do not hear or understand.'
In them is fulfilled the prophecy of Isaiah:
'You will be ever hearing but never understanding; you will be ever seeing but never perceiving.
For this people's heart has become calloused; they hardly hear with their ears, and they have closed their eyes.
Otherwise they might see with their eyes, hear with their ears, understand with their hearts, and turn, and I would heal them.'
But blessed are your eyes because they see, and your ears because they hear.

This passage contains two principles about learning to see the kingdom of God. First, we need Christ's grace, his choosing to reveal to us the secrets of the kingdom. We can only see that which God reveals to us. Because we live under the new covenant, the covenant of the Holy Spirit, we have confidence that God 'will pour out [his] Spirit on all people' (Acts 2:17).

This leads to my second point, which is how we receive kingdom grace. People with soft and teachable hearts openly receive and obey the words of the kingdom. The root problem for people not receiving the secrets of the kingdom is in the heart – our motives and attitudes towards the things of God. But the passage goes on to say that there is a direct relationship between a person's heart and his worldview. A 'hard heart', closed to the supernatural, cannot see or hear the secrets of the kingdom.

There are two ways that a hard heart affects our worldviews. A hard heart may incline us towards a worldview that excludes the supernatural, or it may prevent us from altering a faulty worldview to include the supernatural. In either case, the key to seeing the kingdom of God and doing the works of Christ is opening our hearts more fully to his Spirit. 'What was sown on good soil [an open heart] is the man who hears the word and understands it. He produces a crop, yielding a hundred, sixty, or thirty times what is sown' (Matthew 13:23).

Expectations

We see according to our expectations. Many times our expectations come from conditioning: we are taught to expect certain things in the Christian life, and we miss what God is doing if he acts outside our expectations. In scripture, the story of the feeding of the multitude illustrates how prior conditioning blinds us to learning about the kingdom of God. After Jesus fed thousands, the people said, 'Surely this is the Prophet who is to come into the world' (John 6:14). Jesus withdrew from there because 'they intended to come and make him king by force' (verse 15). The Jews assumed the Messiah was coming to establish an eternal kingdom or to re-establish a political kingdom like David's. Because of this, whenever the people saw a miracle they assumed it must be the Messiah come to establish his political kingdom. Even the disciples, after the resurrection, worked under this assumption (see Acts 1:6). They had the *expectation* of an earthly king.

Years ago I was embarrassed by people in my church who talked about strange, supernatural experiences. Once a lady came to me and described her conversion experience. (She had tried to talk with another pastor about it, but he refused to listen.) She did not fully understand what happened to her and needed help from a pastoral leader. One evening she came home from a party, and on entering her house sensed the presence of someone. It frightened her, but she could not find anyone. Later, in her bedroom, she heard a voice. All it said was 'Rosa Lee'. Her friends knew her only as Lee, even though her full name was Rosa Lee. She turned and saw no one. Then she heard the voice again. This time she asked, 'Who is it? Lord?' 'Yes, Rosa Lee. It is time for you to know me.' She fell on her face and received Christ as her Saviour.

When she told me her story, I thought that she was very strange if not slightly demented. Hearing voices? I took her through biblical steps to salvation, to ensure that she was *really*

saved. She left our meeting hurt. My worldview, my expectations about how God speaks to people today, controlled how I
interpreted her experience, and as a result I cheapened her
conversion experience. (I thank God that years later, after
growing in my understanding of the supernatural, I met her
again and apologised for what I had done. She graciously forgave
me.)

Our expectations are affected by our worldview, our assumptions about the nature of reality. These assumptions also affect
communication, especially our ability to understand language.
Sometimes only slight deviations in how we perceive the world
make great differences. In the second chapter of John's gospel
we read of Jesus taking a whip of cords to businessmen in the
temple courts (verses 13–22). The Jews asked, 'What miraculous
sign can you show us to prove your authority to do all this?' They
were asking for proof that he was the Anointed One. This is not a
surprising question, for the Jews were at the temple, indicating
their devotion and knowledge of scripture. They believed in the
supernatural. Jesus answered, 'Destroy this temple, and I will
raise it again in three days.' Jesus was speaking of his physical
body but the Jews assumed Jesus was speaking about the temple
building in Jerusalem. They could not understand what Jesus
was saying, because, though holding a similar worldview to
Jesus, there was a crucial theological difference between the
two. The Jews could not accept the incarnation. Their theological presuppositions, especially a concern to avoid scrupulously
polytheism, precluded hearing Christ's messianic claims. (Lurking beneath the surface of their theological problem, I suspect,
were hard hearts.)

The Jews held a set of assumptions about the temple: it was
where God was supposed to dwell, a place built out of stone
where they were standing. Based on their knowledge about the
temple, their conclusion that Christ was referring to the temple
building was reasonable. Of what other temple could Jesus have
been speaking? But their knowledge was lacking, forcing the
Jews to draw wrong conclusions. They missed learning a central
truth about the kingdom of God: the Lamb of God must die for
the sins of the world.

In this instance, Jesus was prophesying about his future death
on the cross. He was alluding to the future event of the resurrec-

tion, a sign and the ultimate proof of his authority to clear the temple courts. Only later, after the resurrection, did the disciples understand his words.

Further information and instruction, coming at the crucifixion itself, was the key to interpreting correctly Christ's response to the Jews. This further information altered their assumptions about the temple and Jesus. So correct interpretation was influenced by an experience – a *future* experience at the cross in this instance. Evangelicals believe that experience should not determine theology, that experience must always be subordinated to scripture. While I agree with this, I think there is a sense in which our experience legitimately adds to the interpretation process by altering assumptions, as was the case with Christ's statement to the Jews about the temple.

I have talked with many evangelical theologians who have undergone significant changes in their theology because of an experience. We are always being influenced by our experiences and need the humility to admit it. The question is: what are our criteria for judging these experiences? As we continue to experience Christian living and God, our thinking ought to become more and more scriptural. All too often, though, secularised worldviews filter experience, separating out anything that contradicts modern materialism.

There is another way in which our experience legitimately affects theology. Some truths in scripture cannot be understood until we have had certain experiences. I have found this to be the case with regard to healing. Until I began to experience people being healed, I did not understand many of the scripture passages on healing.

The Bible frequently points us towards experiences that we have not already had, implying that as we have these experiences we will grow in biblical knowledge. Sacrificial love of Christian brothers and sisters and acts of mercy are like that; as we obey, light reflects from our good works back on scripture, revealing more about God's grace and mercy.

So God uses our experiences to show us more fully what he teaches in scripture, many times toppling or altering elements of *our* theology and worldviews. This is what he accomplished with the disciples through their experience of his crucifixion and resurrection. Only then were they able to understand his earlier words at the temple to the Jews: 'Destroy this temple, and I will raise it again in three days.'

Theology

All that I have said about worldviews points towards one conclusion: Christians' worldviews affect their theology. If Christians have a worldview that is affected by Western materialism, they will probably deny that signs and wonders are for today. Though they may use a theological rationale, the real issue is that it upsets their worldview. In contrast to this, a second group of Christians have a worldview that is affected by Western rationalism, they might acknowledge signs and wonders, but consign them to the irrational. These people seek signs and wonders for the thrill of the experience, as an end in themselves. They do not understand the purpose of signs and wonders: to *demonstrate* the kingdom of God.

If we believe in a theology that does not include the possibility of contemporary Christians doing the works of Jesus – including signs and wonders – we will not have a practice of signs and wonders. Kevin Springer knows of a man whose wife was healed after her doctors told him she would not live through the night. The evening the doctors informed him that his wife was terminally ill, he called his church elders, asking them to come and pray for her. The elders were not convinced that God heals today, but nevertheless came out of obligation. They prayed over her, anointing her with oil, and – to their surprise – the next day she walked out of the hospital. The doctors called it 'a miracle'. What is remarkable about this incident is that the elders never told the congregation what happened! They were not as elated as the doctors. Further, this miraculous event did not stimulate the practice of prayer for the sick in the church. Why? Because their theology placed a cloud over an obvious miracle, and they had not developed models for the practice of healing. Even if they openly acknowledged the healing, they would not know how to incorporate the healing ministry in the church. So God healed *in spite* of them; his mercy was greater than the elders' unbelief.

In the last chapter of Acts, we read of Paul being bitten by a viper on the island of Malta. The people from Malta responded first by thinking Paul was a murderer who escaped drowning in the sea but 'Justice [had] not allowed him to live' (verse 4). The Maltese had a cosmic worldview: they assumed interaction between the cosmic and empirical worlds. First they interpreted the viper's bite as God's judgement. Then, seeing Paul alive, they assumed that Paul was a god. For them, only a god would not die from such a bite. The idea that God intervenes directly in the affairs of men and women was an unconscious presupposition.

Secularised people might have said, 'It must have been an old snake' or 'It bit someone earlier in the day and was low on poison'. Western Christians often think the same way, perhaps adding, 'God planned that an old snake would be there in order to save Paul'.

Our assumptions control our conclusions as much as the Maltese people's worldview controlled theirs.[11]

6

THE WORKS OF JESUS

So far I have established three premises that are the basis for power evangelism:
1 Two kingdoms, the kingdom of God and the kingdom of Satan, are in conflict, and Christians have been drafted in Christ's army to do battle against Satan.
2 Evangelism is meant to go forward in the power of the Holy Spirit.
3 Our worldviews affect how we understand scripture, especially passages about signs and wonders.

Keeping this in mind, let us now go on and examine in more detail what Christ did, especially his works of signs and wonders. Jesus' signs and wonders were his calling card, proof that the kingdom of God had come. Theologian Herman Ridderbos writes, 'This factual relation between the coming of the kingdom and Jesus' miracles is brought out not only by the casting out of devils but also by Jesus' other miracles, for they all prove that Satan's power has been broken and that, therefore, the kingdom has come'.[1] Jesus' miracles have another purpose: to show us what the kingdom of God is like, to reveal glimpses of God's love, peace, joy.

Categories of miracles

C. Peter Wagner, in *Church Growth and the Whole Gospel*, outlines two categories of signs of the kingdom found in scripture:
Category A: Social signs, those applied to people in general –
    1 Preaching the good news to the poor
    2 Proclaiming release to the captive
    3 Liberating the oppressed

4 Instituting the Year of Jubilee.

Category B: Personal signs, signs applied to specific individuals –
  1 Restoring sight to the blind
  2 Casting out demons and evil spirits
  3 Healing sick people
  4 Making the lame walk
  5 Cleansing lepers
  6 Restoring hearing to the deaf
  7 Taking up poisonous serpents
  8 Raising the dead
  9 Speaking in tongues
  10 Calming storms
  11 Feeding thousands
  12 Drinking deadly poison with no ill effect.[2]

Describing Category B, Wagner says:

> It is what the Bible refers to when it records the prayers of
> the believers in Jerusalem, 'Stretch out your hand to heal
> and perform miraculous signs and wonders through the
> name of your holy servant Jesus' (Acts 4:30) . . . the main
> function of Category B signs is to draw attention to the
> power of God in order to open unsaved people's hearts to
> the message of the gospel.[3]

Miracles are a foreshadowing and promise of coming universal
redemption and the fullness of the kingdom. Casting out demons
signals God's invasion of the realm of Satan and Satan's final
destruction (Matthew 12:29; Mark 3:27; Luke 11:21ff; John
12:31; Revelation 20:1ff). Healing the sick bears witness to the
end of all suffering (Revelation 21:4). Miraculous provisions of
food tell us about the end of all human need (Revelation 7:16ff).
Stilling storms points forward to the complete victory over the
powers of nature that threaten the earth. Raising the dead
announces that death will be forever done away with (1 Corinthians 15:26).[4]

Jesus himself performed signs and wonders that demonstrated
his reign over these four areas – demons, disease, nature, death.
In each of these power encounters Jesus is doing the works of the
Father, as I describe below.

Demons

In a June 1982 meeting of the Consultation on the Relationship Between Evangelism and Social Responsibility (sponsored by the World Evangelical Fellowship and the Lausanne Committee on World Evangelization), fifty evangelical leaders from twenty-seven different countries gathered in Grand Rapids, Michigan, to discuss social signs of the gospel. In the midst of their final report, we read:

> We believe that signs should validate our evangelism . . . The third sign of the kingdom was exorcism. We refuse to demythologize the teaching of Jesus and his apostles about demons. Although the 'principalities and powers' [see Ephesians 6:12] may have a reference to demonic ideologies and structures, we believe that these certainly are evil personal intelligences under the command of the Devil. Demon possession is a real and terrible condition. Deliverance is possible only in a power encounter in which the name of Jesus is invoked and prevails.[5]

Jesus never met a demon that he liked, and he met them frequently. Demon expulsion is a direct attack by Jesus on Satan, a primary goal of Jesus' mission. 'The reason the Son of God appeared', John wrote in his first letter, 'was to destroy the devil's work' (1 John 3:8). James Dunn writes, 'The binding of Satan was expected by the Jews as a mark of the close of the age.'[6] In this regard the Jews' worldview was similar to Christ's. Jesus came to fulfil that expectation by destroying the works of the Devil and his minions.

Demons exert various degrees of influence over people. In some cases, such as in demonic possession, they gain a high degree of control over the human will. Satan's methods of attack also vary: temptation, inflicting physical and emotional hurt, attempts to kill, demon possession. In scripture, demons cause dumbness (Matthew 9:32–33), physical blindness (Matthew 12:22–23), and epilepsy (Matthew 17:14–21). Mental insanity is suggested in Mark 5, where the healed Gerasene demoniac is described as clothed and in his right mind, suggesting that before he was not. Of course, not *all* (or even most) physical, emotional, and psychological problems are caused by Satan; however, in some instances they may be caused by him.

Jesus withstood Satan's attacks in the wilderness, then immediately taught that the rule of God was near (Mark 1:15). Soon after his wilderness temptation, during his first sermon (in the synagogue at Capernaum), Jesus cast out a demon from a man (Mark 1:21–28). Before being cast out, the demon enquired, 'Have you come to destroy us'? This question reveals a knowledge of what God has in store for them at the end of the age. Jesus, through his actions, demonstrated that he had come to destroy them, though that destruction will not be accomplished fully until the age to come.

Jesus told the demon to 'come out of him' and 'be quiet'. The former phrase is frequently translated, 'He rebuked him'. It means to denounce or censure in order to end an action. What he said was 'Stop it! That's enough!' 'Be quiet' conveys the idea of strangling or muting. He throttled the demon, and the demon left. Jesus saw the man as a victim of an unseen force, and Christ ruthlessly dealt with the spirit.

The disciples expelled demons. We also advance the kingdom of God in the same way: overthrowing every contrary spirit in the name of our King. Too many Christians do not know how to deal with demons. They are afraid of evil spirits. They do not understand the scriptural basis for our authority and power over them. We can and ought to treat evil spirits ruthlessly – binding, rebuking, and casting them out whenever we encounter them.

Authority over demons is power that Christ freely gives Christians. When the seventy returned from their missions, they said, 'Lord, even the demons submit to us in your name'. Christ responded, 'I saw Satan fall like lightning from heaven. I have given you authority to trample on snakes and scorpions, and to overcome all the power of the enemy; nothing will harm you' (Luke 10:17–19). There is no doubt that we possess all the authority we need to overcome demons (Mark 16:17–18; Acts 1:8; Revelation 12:11). Jesus was acknowledging the battle that we have been thrown into on earth, and that God had thrown Satan out of heaven but we need not fear his power to hurt.

Several years ago I spoke at a conference in York, England. After one of the meetings I was introduced to a girl with serious demonic problems. She was twenty-five years old and since the age of three had been tormented by evil spirits. She suffered from severe curvature of the spine, metabolic problems that caused her to give off offensive odours, and an assortment of psychological problems. She was in constant physical and emotional pain. But she wanted freedom from her bondage.

Her story was sad indeed. Molested since the age of six, she had been in and out of institutions all her life. She had even developed a 'theology' that rationalised drug abuse and sexual perversion.

For seven hours we prayed over her, eventually casting out forty-seven demons. She was then able to repent of her sin and receive Christ as Lord and Saviour. Her life was immediately changed, though for several years she required extensive pastoral counselling. Released from Satan's bondage, she was able to deal with these problems. In 1984 she married a Christian and today is doing well, living the normal Christian life.

Disease

One of Satan's most effective works is disease. Almost half of all the verses in three of the gospels are about healing. Yet too often we read these accounts through the filters of modern scientism, assuming physical disease has only a physical cause and solution. Subconsciously or consciously, we read of healings in the New Testament and assume that either they were only for the early church or there is another explanation – a scientific one – for how these healings actually occurred. For this reason, for years the only prayer for healing that I practised was 'Lord, guide the surgeon's hands'. I still pray that sometimes, but I have many more options now.

Causes of disease may be physical, psychological, spiritual. Regardless of the cause, though, Christians have power over disease. Christians in the first century saw disease as a work of Satan, a weapon of his demons, a way in which evil rules the world. When Jesus healed disease, whether demonically or physically caused, he pushed back the kingdom of Satan. There was nothing the devil did that Jesus did not undo.

In Luke 13 we read of a woman – crippled for eighteen years – who was healed by Jesus (verses 10–17). Jesus called her forward and said, 'Woman, you are set free from your infirmity'. She had been incarcerated by Satan, and Jesus was setting the captive free. 'Then he put his hands on her, and immediately she straightened up and praised God'.

In response to attacks from the Pharisees (because Jesus healed her on the sabbath, a day of rest for the Jews), Jesus said, 'You hypocrites! . . . should not this woman, a daughter of Abraham, *whom Satan has kept bound for eighteen long years*, be set free?' His was not a medical explanation. He put the root of her problems at Satan's feet. The Pharisees operated with hardness of heart and religious blindness. They hid behind theology, in this case involving the prohibition of work on the sabbath.

During Christ's time, Edward Langton asserts in his book *Essentials of Demonology*, 'Special demons came to be associated with particular forms of disease or sickness. Certain diseases were held to be caused by particular demons'.[7] Again, not *all* cases of disease are caused by demons or are demons. Often, of course, there are psychological or physical explanations for illness. But more frequently than many Western Christians realise, the cause is demonic.

Seeing demons as a possible cause of disease is difficult to accept, because it challenges modern, materialistic notions about disease and infirmity. In Jesus' day, his explanation – 'Satan has kept [her] bound' – was accepted easily. Not even the Pharisees questioned it. Today, most Western people assume that her curvature of the spine was rooted in an accident or developmental problem. Yet, whatever the means, Jesus thought Satan was the cause. We have been called to deal with the cause, not with how Satan inflicts disease and suffering.

Western Christians all too often look at disease and infirmity and accept it, saying, 'It must be the will of God' or 'We'll understand it better when we get to heaven'. In some cases God *doesn't* heal. But frequently people make these statements to mean God doesn't *want* to heal anyone today. In this sense, these statements are platitudes, falling short of what God has for us. He is a God of mercy and love, and has given us the authority to work the works of Jesus.

Recently, while in Johannesburg, South Africa, I was asked to pray over a fourteen-year-old Zulu boy who had not grown an inch since the age of seven. His fingers and toes were practically missing; his jaw broken, and teeth ruined; he was incapable of speaking or walking (his mother carried him to the meeting). I was deeply saddened when I saw him.

When I spoke to him, he responded – in perfect English! I had been told that he could not talk, and if he could it would not have been in English. I knew then that I was dealing with a demon.

So I called over several other Christians, people who I knew were experienced in deliverance, and we began praying over the boy. While praying, a member of the group discerned that a curse was on him. Someone had called demons on him when he was younger, asking them to torment and kill the boy. It was not clear who spoke the curse, but it seemed to be the source of his problems. We broke the power of the curse by speaking against it in the name of Christ, and then cast out several demons who were afflicting him.

Later we learned that when he was seven years old, living in another town, the boy had been a runner for a witch doctor, his aunt. His mother decided to move. Because the witch doctor was losing his service, she placed a curse on the child. The day the aunt placed the curse on the boy, the mother returned home to find him in a degenerated, animal-like condition. Over the years his condition had grown worse, until we encountered him in Johannesburg.

The results of breaking the curse were remarkable. Within two days, the boy returned to the meetings, walking and able to recognise me. We prayed over him again, and his many sores were healed. Many of the people who attended the meetings were converted to Christianity because of his healing.

After we left South Africa, other Christians followed up with regular prayer. Four months later, he returned home (he had been institutionalised). He enrolled in school, and in several months advanced two grade levels.

In Luke we find the story of Peter's mother-in-law's healing (Luke 4:38–9). Jesus, scripture reports, 'Rebuked the fever'. This is the same language that Jesus used to drive the demon out of the man in the synagogue at Capernaum. Apparently the origin of the mother-in-law's fever was a demon. She was healed instantly. Jesus frequently spoke the same way to fevers as he did to demons, because he saw an integral unity between sickness and Satan.

Another tool for healing is God's forgiveness. When the paralytic was lowered through the roof in Capernaum, Jesus said, 'Son, your sins are forgiven' (Mark 2:5). In response to the Pharisees' attack on him for forgiving the paralytic's sin, Jesus asks, 'Which is easier: to say to the paralytic "Your sins are forgiven," or to say, "Get up, take your mat and walk"'? He then healed the paralytic. Obviously forgiveness of sins is a far greater miracle, for it opens the door to eternal life – the goal and purpose for signs and wonders.

There is great power in forgiveness of sin. In 1984 I spoke at a conference in the midwest of the United States. After one of the meetings, in the parking lot, I met a woman who suffered with crippling arthritis. Her pain was so great that she needed a walker to get about. I talked with her before praying and discovered that her husband had abandoned her and her daughter fourteen years earlier, and it was shortly thereafter that her arthritic problems began. She also told me – and her daughter (who was with her) – that her husband had run off with another man. She had kept this information from her daughter all these years.

On hearing this, I became enraged at what Satan had done, and said, 'That's enough'! Here was an instance when the Holy Spirit stirred my heart, showing me that the source of arthritis was her yielding to Satan's unrelenting slandering of her husband, and her resultant bitterness towards her husband and God. I was enraged by what Satan had done, and so was the Holy Spirit.

When I spoke those two words (they almost exploded out of me), the power of God fell on the woman. Her body trembled violently; her joints changed shape – fingers and legs strengthened. Satan's grip, the power of bitterness and accusation, was broken. Then she confessed her sin of harbouring bitterness towards her husband and God. I reassured her of God's forgiveness. That night she was healed of about eighty percent of her condition. More prayer was needed for the other twenty percent. Sin that finds safe harbour in our bodies is capable of all sorts of physical damage. Receiving forgiveness was a key to her healing.

Nature

Just as demonic forces play havoc in the lives of men and women through sickness and demonisation, they can also exert their perverted influence by causing nature to run amuck.

In the fourth chapter of Mark's gospel, Jesus wars on nature – in this case on 'a furious squall' and waves that threatened to swamp his and the disciples' boat as they crossed a lake. This story is often used to illustrate inward harmony for Christians as they encounter the various winds and waves of life's challenges. While this analogy may be true, it overlooks the primary intent of the author, which is to show Jesus ruling over nature itself.

Western materialists find Christ's rule over nature impossible to accept. They see Christ's calming of the seas as a fantastic story, smacking of animism, suggesting primitive religion, even superstition. The equating of *all* natural calamity with evil spirits would be animism. But simply acknowledging the possibility of Satan's influence in nature, and Christ's lordship over that influence, is not animism.

Christians also succumb to rationalism, thinking, 'Well, that's Christ's divinity ruling over natural forces – it doesn't relate to how we live today'. Yet the Bible teaches that Jesus performed works of miracles to demonstrate that he had the authority and power to do so, and that his power is available to us to do the same works.

The disciples in the boat were experienced fishermen. They knew the waters and thought that they were going to die. 'Teacher', they said, 'don't you care if we drown'? After calming the storm, Jesus rebuked them for being afraid and lacking faith. Jesus' response used to puzzle me. Was not their fear reasonable, considering the circumstances? Then one day, while I was sitting beside the Sea of Galilee and meditating on this passage, the opening words of the text came to mind: 'He said to his disciples, "Let us go over to the other side"' (verse 35). The same person who said, 'Let there be light' said, 'Let us go over to the other side.' When he asked, 'Do you still have no faith?' it was because he had already declared that they were going to the other side.

The sure knowledge of the Father's will gave Jesus the liberty to sleep soundly while crossing, even during a storm. The disciples had to awaken him!

The words that Jesus used to calm the lake are similar to those used to overcome demons and disease. He saw a unity in this situation between Satan's and nature's attacks. This was a classic power encounter in which Jesus was at war with the perpetrator of destruction.

Death

'The end will come', taught Paul, 'when [Jesus] hands over the kingdom to God the Father after he has destroyed all dominion, authority, and power. For he must reign until he has put all his enemies under his feet. *The last enemy to be destroyed is death*' (1 Corinthians 15:24–26). Jesus hated death – Satan's most fearful weapon – because it is final.

Unlike deliverance from evil spirits, which Christ appeared to perform every time he encountered a willing person; and healing, which he did with great frequency; resuscitation was infrequent. Bur the miracles of resuscitation have enormous significance. The gospels record three specific and one general account of his raising the dead.[8] These miracles strike Satan at his greatest point of strength and signal that his reign was broken by Jesus.

In Luke 7 Jesus raised from the dead a widow's son (verses 11 to 17). Coming to the town of Nain, he encountered the widow's son's funeral procession. Luke wrote, 'When the Lord saw her, his heart went out to her and he said, "Don't cry"'. He then commanded her son to get up. The crowd's response was to exclaim that 'God has come to help his people'.

Jesus is the embodiment of his Father, of the same nature, functioning in perfect concert with his will for the redemption of the human race. The Father's will is to help people, to extend compassion and mercy. Resuscitation assured the people that God loved them, and that some day even death would be overcome.

SIGNS AND WONDERS IN THE EARLY CHURCH

When first-century Christians came to a new town, signs and wonders followed. Starting at Pentecost, power evangelism swept the Mediterranean, demonstrating that the kingdom of God meets every human need. From Jerusalem to Rome, from Asia to Europe; among Jews, Samaritans, and Gentiles; in every town, culture, and race, God's rule was established. We should not be surprised at this: a major part of Christ's ministry was devoted to training the disciples to do the Father's works, preparing them to lead the church that was created at Pentecost.

But Christ's method of training is difficult for Western Christians to understand. There are several reasons for this. Evangelicals emphasise accumulating knowledge about God through Bible study. Christ was more action orientated. His disciples learned by doing as he did.

I have always found it rather odd that scientific Bible study, the historical-critical method, was not a key element in Christ's method of discipleship. Odd, because scientific Bible study is the foremost, if not exclusive, method of training among Western evangelicals today, especially in our seminaries. The historical-critical method employs historical study, linguistics, and historical theology to discover what scripture meant to its first-century audience. The method rightly assumes that what God intended to say to first-century Christians is what he intends for us also.

But there are problems related to the historical-critical method and the discipleship process. The first is that reliance on an intellectual method, within a classroom-orientated structure, skews the goal of the discipleship process towards intellectual formation and away from moral and spiritual formation. As we

shall see, Christ's method of training was rabbinic, more orientated towards learning a way of life through doing than through
the accumulation of knowledge about God.

The second problem is that evangelicals tend to rely on this
method alone for character formation. This leads to an intellectual understanding of Christianity. If the historical-critical
method were used as one tool among many, there might not be
the tendency towards intellectualisation of the Christian faith.
But this is not usually the case.

'The historical-critical method,' says New Testament scholar
Russell P. Spittler, 'when applied to scripture, is both legitimate
and necessary – but inadequate . . . inadequate because . . . the
end of biblical study cannot consist of historical dates or tenta-
tive judgements about complicated and conjectured literary origins. The end of biblical study consists rather in enhanced faith,
hope, and love both for the individual and the community. The
historical-critical method is inadequate, in other words, because
it does not address piety'. For Spittler, an important element of
piety is God speaking to him through scripture and prayer.[1]

The last problem involves the effect the historical-critical
method has on the process of Bible study. Scripture study needs
to proceed in the spirit of faith, hope, and love. By its nature, the
historical-critical method is a rigorous intellectual task. The
student easily falls into reliance on study instead of reliance on
the Holy Spirit.

Christ based his training on scripture, and the goal of his
training was piety, learning to hear God's voice and do his
bidding.

Among Western Christians, another obstacle to understanding Christ's method of discipleship is the rejection of signs and
wonders today. Signs and wonders, all Western evangelicals
acknowledge, were necessary to authenticate Christ's divinity.
Further, signs and wonders were key in establishing the apostolic
authority of the twelve and Paul. But most Western Christians
reject or adopt a generally negative attitude towards signs and
wonders after the first century. This diminishes the effectiveness
of Christ's example for us, discounting much of what Christ
intended that we do. What Christians – including evangelicals –
are often left to follow is a good moral example, not a dynamic,
Satan-conquering Lord. This results in overly intellectual dis-

ciples – certainly not a people who cause demons to tremble.

A closer look at how Jesus trained the disciples to do signs and wonders, and how they carried on that ministry after Christ's ascension, reveals many of the key elements for practising power evangelism today.

A motley crew

Signs and wonders were the proof of Jesus' messiahship, the calling cards of the kingdom of God. Their presence in the early church demonstrates that Jesus intended them to be an integral part of the disciples' ministry.

The disciples learned from Jesus how to do the works of the kingdom. They might not have always understood the purpose of his miracles, but they learned how to do signs and wonders with remarkable success. Jesus' method of instruction was the method of the day: rabbinic. A rabbi would minister while his disciples watched, then they would minister with him watching; next they went out on short missions, reporting back for further instruction and correction from the master. After repeating this process for years, when the rabbi was convinced his disciples were formed in *his* way of life, he released his students to repeat this process with others.

Christ used this same training method with his disciples. Christ, the Teacher, Rabbi, formed his disciples in *his* way of life, passing on his character. Faith, hope, love, joy, peace, and so on were the goals of his training. Signs and wonders – casting out demons, healing the sick, even walking on water – were avenues through which the disciples learned more about God's nature.

The disciples understood and accepted what Jesus expected of them. We never read of them objecting to being *asked* to do the works of Jesus, only of their sense of personal insufficiency in performing his commands.

In the early years of my upbringing I often visited a horse farm in Illinois where my grandfather worked. He trained Tennessee walking horses. Tennessee walkers have a remarkable, high-strutting gait, different from any other breed of horse in the world. One day I was with him while he worked on a horse with a problem gait. His solution was to hitch a pacer – a horse with an orthodox gait – to the horse with the problem, and let them walk together. After a few days, the problem horse's gait became consistent, just like the pacer's. My grandfather explained that when a horse cannot do its job, connect it to one that can, and soon both do the job correctly.

I have been training men and women for twenty-five years. During this period I have learned that the secret for success with people is the same as with horses: hitch a person who cannot do a job with one who can, and soon both will know how. This is how Christ trained the Twelve: they lived with him, soon living like him. Power evangelism works the same way. Being around someone who does it successfully is the best way to learn to do it yourself.

The primary criterion that Christ had for choosing the Twelve was a willingness to follow him – to walk with him, choosing to become like him. Other than that desire, the disciples' only common characteristics were their Jewishness, Galilean up-bringing, and lower-middle class economic and social standing. (Judas was the exception.) From a human perspective, one can imagine the Father telling his Son, 'If we can train this motley crew to advance my kingdom, we can train anyone'. This gives all of us hope.

Through mutual commitment, Jesus made disciples out of the Twelve. He developed mature character and leadership in them. He trained them to do signs and wonders. They were hitched together for three years, and when released the disciples continued to walk in his way. They performed signs and wonders, and trained the next generation to perform them also.

But the disciples had difficulty in learning to do signs and wonders. They often misunderstood Christ's teachings (Matthew 13:36; 15:15; 16:6–12). They never fully understood his mission until after the resurrection – and even then they were in need of further correction (Mark 8:31–32; 9:31–32; Acts 1:6). They also misunderstood his authority as it related to the kingdom of God (Mark 10:35–40; Luke 9:46–48). But Jesus was patient with them, for his goal was to build men who did the Father's bidding.

For three years, the Twelve were in a learning environment. They not only learned new ideas but they developed new skills and abilities. They were teachable because they saw a large gap between Christ's life and their own. A process of progressive growth came through trial and error.

Frequent failures characterised the early ministry of all the disciples (Luke 9:37–43, 52–55). This was especially true of Peter's life. His abortive attempt to walk on water, found in Matthew 14, is one of many examples. As the disciples continued to live with Christ, their failures diminished, their successes becoming more frequent. Each new step of faith was a springboard for their Master to push them further, stretching their worldviews, expanding their understanding of God.

Faith in the miraculous

Perhaps the most difficult lesson the disciples learned was how to have faith that produces miracles. Maybe I am overly sensitive to this because I had such difficulty learning about this type of faith. I think not, though.

For example, consider the feeding of the 5,000 found in Mark 6:33–44. This is one of the greatest miracles in the New Testament. There are several points about faith to learn from this episode in order to practise power evangelism.

First, Jesus was motivated by compassion. 'When Jesus landed and saw a large crowd', verse 34 states, 'he had compassion on them, because they were like sheep without a shepherd'. Jesus' divine compassion and supernatural mercy frequently precipitated his works. (Moved with compassion, he healed, taught, performed miracles, raised the dead, expelled demons. See Matthew 20:33; Mark 1:41; 5:19; 6:34; 8:2–10; Luke 7:11–17.) We too need to ask God for his compassion.

Second, Jesus, listening to his Father, did not yield to the apostles' wish to send the crowd away. The apostles, observing the people's hunger and their lack of immediate resources, concluded that the crowd should be dispersed (verses 35 to 36). Their insight was quite reasonable; they gave no thought to a miraculous provision. But if Jesus had acceded to their suggestion to disperse, one of the greatest miracles recorded in scripture would have been lost. I wonder how many times we 'rationally and reasonably' miss miracles today? Jesus listened to the Father – not the disciples – and the miracle was performed.

Third, Jesus used the disciples' spiritual blindness as an occasion to train them in signs and wonders. 'You give them something to eat' was his response to their suggestion to disperse the crowd. This, of course, gave the apostles cause to re-examine their resources: five loaves and two fish. It was a crucial moment in their training. They were being told to do something for which they did not have adequate resources. I have discovered that praying for the healing of a blind person accomplishes the same thing in me. I know my own resources are inadequate. Miracles occur through our inadequacy, the crucible in which faith is formed.

Fourth, Jesus gave instructions to the disciples, and they obeyed. He told them to organise the crowd 'in groups of hundreds and fifties' (verse 40). They had no idea from where the food was to come, nevertheless they prepared the people to receive. We are in the same position today: we need to listen to and act on Jesus' instructions, even when we cannot see the provision.

Finally, the miracle of multiplication of the bread and fish probably occurred in the apostles' hands as well as Christ's. He had commanded the apostles to 'give them something to eat' (verse 37). Many commentators believe that the miracle of multiplication occurred only in the hands of Jesus. They may be correct. The passage leaves room for thinking the miracle happened in the disciples' hands as well as Christ's – just as with exorcism and healing.

It is a possible interpretation that the apostles were handed, after Christ's blessing, a meagre portion of bread and fish. Then they went into the crowd and began passing it out, with the multiplication occurring before their eyes. The miracle was in their hands and hearts. They learned that multiplication could occur through them. Only God can work miracles, but he often does it in the hands of Christians.

We must do better than the apostles in learning from this miracle. Later, after Jesus walked on the water, Mark says, 'They were completely amazed, for they had not understood about the loaves; their hearts were hardened' (Mark 6:51–52). Jesus had to show the twelve again and again how to perform signs and wonders. With the help of the Holy Spirit and with soft hearts, we can avoid some of their failures.

Transferring ministry

In Luke 9 we read, 'When Jesus had called the Twelve together, he gave them power and authority to drive out all demons and to cure diseases, and he sent them out to preach the kingdom of God and to heal the sick' (verses 1–2). He was sending the disciples as his personal ambassadors, thus they went in his authority and power.

Their commissioning is analogous to being train drivers. Train drivers direct powerful machines, and success depends on working within specific schedules, tracks, and speeds. Too often we think the authority and power of God is a carte blanche to do whatever we want, more like driving an automobile as opposed to a train. In fact, the commission to the twelve came with stringent limitations: they were only to do the will of the Father.

When he sent them, Jesus provided the disciples with practical instructions. He told them where and to whom they should go. They were to proclaim the kingdom of God to its recipients, freely offering healing – no matter what the needs – because they themselves had received freely. A simple lifestyle of trusting God and owning few material possessions (for freedom of movement) was observed. They received hospitality and material support from people receptive to their message, and avoided wasting time with those who rejected the kingdom. Persecution was expected, so they were taught to operate wisely yet keep their innocence (not an easy task, though Christ's life was their pattern). In all instances Jesus' Spirit would help and instruct them.

Even though given the authority and power of the kingdom of God, the twelve still had to exercise it. Power, I too have learned, comes as we exercise what God has given. The disciples could give only what they had received, but in giving they received more. Until they had actually healed the sick and cast out demons, their authority and power meant little to them.

The twelve encountered difficulties, though at first their excursions were successful – even the demons were subject to them! Soon, however, they faced difficulties with their own pride and carnality. For example, they tried to stop others who were healing in Jesus' name, and lapsed into unbelief. They also experienced persecution from religious leaders.

In the ninth chapter of Luke, we read of Christ's response to the disciples' failure, in this case their inability to cast a demon from a child. 'O unbelieving and perverse generation, how long shall I stay with you and put up with you?' (verse 41). Jesus was frustrated by their lack of faith. It was very important to him that they learn how to cast out all demons, so that when he departed from earth that ministry would continue.

Christ delivered the boy of the evil spirit immediately, using the occasion to teach the disciples that soon they would not have his help. 'Listen carefully to what I am about to tell you: The Son of Man is going to be betrayed into the hands of men' (verse 44). They needed to learn about faith for deliverance, because he was soon to leave them.

Signs and wonders were done through the followers' faith, quickened by the guidance of the Holy Spirit. When with Jesus, the disciples were trained in faith for miracles. When Peter and John healed the lame man at the gate called Beautiful, Peter explained that it was not because of their spirituality; faith in Jesus' name made the man whole (Acts 3:1–10). This assertive faith has confidence without need of proof or regard for evidence, a willingness to stand by what God commands. (I do not imply that we claim someone is healed when symptoms of illness are still present. Faith for healing means that we believe God is able to heal specific persons today, and that there is a specific sense of God's working.)

The expansion of the ministry of signs and wonders from the One to many has cosmic effects. When Jesus sent out the twelve, and later the seventy, he increased the possibilities for people's deliverance from the Devil. The kingdom of darkness suffered defeat. The expansion of the kingdom of God – and accompanying defeat of Satan – is effected by the number of Christians performing signs and wonders.

Accompanying signs

For three years Jesus taught the disciples how to minister from hearts of compassion and mercy, hear the Father, grow in dependence on the Holy Spirit, be obedient to God's leading, and believe that God performs miracles through men and women. Even though they frequently forgot or misunderstood what they were taught, his post-resurrection commission, as recorded in Mark 16, was consistent with their training:

> Jesus appeared to the Eleven as they were eating; he rebuked them for their lack of faith . . . [and he] said to them, 'Go into all the world and preach the good news to all creation . . . and these signs will accompany those who believe: In my name they will drive out demons; they will speak in new tongues; they will pick up snakes with their hands; and when they drink deadly poison, it will not hurt them at all; they will place their hands on sick people, and they will get well.' . . . Then the disciples went out and preached everywhere, and the Lord worked with them and confirmed his word by the signs that accompanied it (Mark 16:14–20).

I find it remarkable that many Western Christians are surprised at the emphasis on signs and wonders in this commissioning. Yet the way the disciples fulfilled the great commission indicates Christ's commitment to power evangelism, a key part of their training.

Some have challenged the canonicity of Mark 16:9–20. While it is true that two of the most reliable early manuscripts do not contain this passage, all Christian traditions have included it in the canon of scripture. But even if the passage is excluded from the canon, we cannot disregard the overwhelming evidence that the early disciples in fact fulfilled the Marcan commission: they cast out demons, spoke in tongues, picked up snakes, and healed the sick.

Luke was the theologian of the Holy Spirit. In the first chapter of Acts, he wrote that Acts was a companion volume to his gospel. The purpose of his gospel was to write all that Jesus did and taught (Acts 1:1). In Acts, Luke continued the story of Jesus' works and teaching, only now he worked through the disciples (Acts 1:8).

Luke began the book of Acts by contrasting the disciples before Pentecost with the empowered group after. In chapter one, the disciples still operated according to Old Testament principles. They misunderstood Christ's mission (verse 6); they chose Judas' replacement by casting lots, recalling the Urim and

Thummim of the Old Testament. After the Spirit came, and again someone needed to be chosen to fill an office, they used different methods (see Acts 6:1–6). The training they received in discipleship came together with the catalytic outpouring of God's Spirit at Pentecost. Power evangelism was unleashed on the world.

There are at least ten kinds of sign phenomena in the book of Acts that produced evangelistic growth in the church. They were specifically called 'signs and wonders' nine times, and are the most frequent sign phenomena in the book of Acts. They included healing, expelling demons, miracles with nature and food, resuscitation of the dead, being transported from one place to another. In chapter 5 we read, 'The apostles performed many miraculous signs and wonders among the people . . . more and more men and women believed in the Lord and were added to their number' (verses 12 and 14).[2] One power encounter is mentioned, between Paul and Elymas in Salamis, on the island of Cyprus. The result was that the proconsul believed (13:4–12). The following is an incomplete summary, though I have added footnotes with more detailed references for further investigation:

1 *Speaking gifts*. Tongues and prophecy occur four times in Acts, three in which the church grew. For example, at Pentecost the disciples were 'filled with the Holy Spirit and began to speak in other tongues as the Spirit enabled them', resulting in 'about three thousand [being] added to their number that day' (2:4, 41).[3]

2 *Visions*. There are four instances of visions. Cornelius, the Caesarean centurion, received a vision – an answer to his prayers – and was told to send for Peter. The next day, Peter had a related vision. The two visions resulted in the gospel being preached to the Gentiles for the first time, with many responding in baptism (see 10:3, 9–12, 47).[4]

3 *Dead raised*. There are two resuscitations recorded. The first case was that of Dorcas (or Tabitha, as she was called in Aramaic), in which Peter raised her from the dead, resulting in 'many people [believing] in the Lord' (9:40–42). In the second instance Paul raised Eutychus from the dead, with no recorded evangelistic result (20:7–12).

4 *Assorted miracles*. There are six specific miracles recorded.

On the island of Malta a viper bit Paul, with Paul suffering no ill effects. According to church tradition, the people responded to the miracle by believing in Christ, and the church was established (28:3–10).[5]

There were also phenomena that were likened to miracles of nature. For example the gates opening for Peter in chapter 12; the earthquake, unfastened fetters, and opened doors in chapter 16; and the sound like wind and tongues like fire in chapter two. The last two phenomena helped account for 3,000 converts.

5 *Healings.* There are seven specific healings. In chapter 9, we read of Paul healing Aeneas's paralysis, resulting in the conversion of the towns of Lydda and Sharon (verses 32–43).[6]

6 *Angelic visitations.* There are three recorded visitations. In chapter 8 an angel told Philip to go to a desert road south of Jerusalem. There he evangelised the Ethiopian eunuch (verses 26 to 40). According to church tradition, the eunuch returned to Ethiopia and established the church.[7]

Signs and wonders occurred fourteen times in the book of Acts in conjunction with preaching, resulting in church growth.[8] Further, on twenty occasions church growth was a direct result of signs and wonders performed by the disciples. Rarely was church growth attributed to preaching alone.

What conclusions can be drawn from my brief survey of the books of Acts? First, the early church – particularly the Twelve – carried on Christ's ministry, including signs and wonders. They were trained by Christ in how to do them, and they did them well.

Second, more than the twelve healed the sick, cast out demons, experienced visions. Other Christians did. Signs and wonders were a part of daily life, expected by the church. Paul, Stephen, Cornelius, Ananias – none of them the original Twelve – all practised signs and wonders.

Finally, signs and wonders resulted in dramatic church growth. They were the catalyst for evangelism.

Signs and wonders and church history

Signs and wonders did not cease with the close of the New Testament canon. They have continued to occur throughout history. Reliable documents from every century of church history demonstrate that prophecy, healing, deliverance, and tongues have not disappeared from the Christian experience (see Appendices A and B).

Among theologians and historians today we find a variety of perspectives on the validity of signs and miracles. These positions influence how writers treat reports of miracles. J. Sidlow Baxter, in his book, *Divine Healing of the Body*, describes four positions with regard to signs and wonders in post-biblical history, held by modern Christians.[9]

1 *Signs and wonders ceased at the end of the apostolic age, around the end of the first century.* Reformed theologian B. B. Warfield, in his book *Counterfeit Miracles*, thought the supernatural gifts 'were confined to the apostolic age, and to a very narrow circle then'. Their purpose was to establish the authority of the apostles; once accomplished, the charismatic gifts were done away with.

According to Warfield's position, signs and wonders reported after that time were, a priori, either spurious or did not occur by divine means. This is a circular argument, in which a theological judgement is made that signs and wonders are impossible after the first century, forcing the conclusion that historical evidence is fraudulent. The great weakness of Warfield's position is he cannot use scripture to support his contention that divine miracles ceased on the death of the apostles and their generation. No scripture either states or implies his position. (For a discussion of 1 Corinthians 13:10, see chapter eight.)

2 *Signs and wonders ceased because they belonged only to the earliest centuries of the church.* According to this theory, they were no longer needed to validate the gospel. The church, once widely established and officially sanctioned, was enough to certify the authenticity of the Christian message. The cut-off date is the time of the completion of the canon – usually recognised to have been at the Council of Carthage in 397.

This argument accepts second- and third-century documentation of signs and wonders, arbitrarily assigning their early cessation. But why a particular cut-off? When was the church widely established and officially sanctioned? Is 397 when the canon was closed? (Many historians would dispute that conclusion.)

3 *Signs and wonders faded and ceased as leaders of the organised*

church came against them. This argument, which contradicts the church-establishment theories above, has some merit. In fact, as faith for miracles wanes, especially among pastoral leaders, miracles decrease in frequency. Also, when unusual signs and wonders have occurred – events that often threaten the hierarchy and status quo of the church – leadership has tended to inhibit them.

There have been waves of signs and wonders throughout church history, with the hierarchy alternately retarding or encouraging their ebb and flow. But the main point of this argument – that the gifts have completely ceased – cannot stand up to the historical test. It cannot be documented that the gifts have ceased for any significant period of time in church history, especially today.

4 *Signs and wonders have never ceased.* They have occurred from the apostolic age until now, in varying degrees. This last position is supported by scripture and church history.

After the Enlightenment – and with the advent of nineteenth-century theological liberalism – church leaders have resisted signs and wonders. They denied the *possibility* of supernatural intervention in creation. Theological secularists, as I prefer to call them, do not fit into any of Baxter's categories. They deny the possibility of even first-century signs and wonders. They are, sadly, materialists cloaking their philosophy with religious language.

How have positions that deny signs and wonders become popular among Western Christians, including orthodox, historic Christians? Why the scepticism or overt ridicule towards reports of miracles? The next chapter tells why.

8

THE NEXT STAGE

C. Peter Wagner, in a 1983 interview, predicted a new stage (or third wave, as he calls it) of the Holy Spirit's work in this century. The first, Dr. Wagner noted, was the Pentecostal movement at the turn of the century. The second began in the 1960s, popularly known as the charismatic renewal, touching mainline Protestants and Catholics. He predicted a third wave washing evangelical Protestants.[1]

I believe Dr. Wagner's 'third wave' is not so much another wave as the next stage of development in the charismatic renewal. Perhaps both the Pentecostal and charismatic movements are part of one great move of the Holy Spirit in this century. This perspective emphasises the similarities of the movements, which outweigh their differences.

There is much to learn from the first two movements in this century. 'If it weren't for the charismatic movement and the classical Pentecostals', Dr. Wagner noted, 'we who are neither one of those would probably never have even heard of the power of the Holy Spirit. So what we are doing is certainly attributable to the way in which God is working in them. What I see is a lowering of traditional barriers between those of us who are evangelicals, and charismatics and Pentecostals, so that we can have the same results, the same work of the Holy Spirit in both groups, even though we tend to explain what is happening in a slightly different way'.[2]

In preparation for my course at Fuller Seminary on The Miraculous and Church Growth, I studied both the Pentecostal and charismatic movements. I discovered why, despite holding a similar theology, the two are different: each of these movements has affected different groups of people. These groups are culled from different economic, social, religious, and educational pools. As would be expected, the nature of each movement is quite different.

Pentecostalism

The modern Pentecostal movement started at the April 1906 Azusa Street revival in Los Angeles, California. Thomas Ball Barratt (the 'apostle of Pentecost' to Western Europe) brought the Azusa Street revival back to his church in Oslo, Sweden, in December 1906. From there it spread quickly to the United Kingdom. For church growth in this century Pentecostals far outstrip all other Christian groups. Of the 345,000,000 Protestants worldwide by 1980 Pentecostals comprised the largest denominational subgroup, with over 51,000,000 members. (There are 49,800,000 Anglicans, 47,550,000 Baptists, 43,360,000 Lutherans.)[3]

Growth in individual Pentecostal denominations and churches highlights this trend. For example, beginning in 1914 with about 10,000 members, the Assemblies of God currently claims over 10,000,000 members worldwide.[4] Since 1964, the Church of God in Christ, the largest predominantly black Pentecostal denomination in America, has grown from 450,000 to 3,710,000 members.[5] According to church growth specialist Elmer Towns, four of the ten largest congregations in the world are now Pentecostal, including the three largest: the Full Gospel Central Church (500,000) in Seoul, Korea; the Jotabeche Church (100,000) in Santiago, Chile; and the Congregacao Crista (61,250) in Sao Paulo, Brazil.[6]

Not only do these statistics indicate spectacular growth but missiologists believe the Pentecostals could grow much larger. For example, in Latin America C. Peter Wagner projects that Pentecostal numbers could increase *five-fold* over the next fifteen years. (In 1969, sixty-three percent of all Latin American Protestants were Pentecostals.[7]) Here is the overall Protestant trend in Latin America:

In 1900 there were about 50,000 Protestants in all of Latin America.
In the 1930s growth passed the one million mark.

In the 1940s growth passed the two million mark.
In the 1950s growth passed the five million mark.
In the 1960s growth passed the ten million mark.
In the 1970s growth passed the twenty million mark.

Some statisticians project around 100 million Protestants in Latin America for the year 2,000.[8]

Dr. Wagner believes the Pentecostal proportion has increased since 1969, meaning there could be between 65,000,000 and 75,000,000 Pentecostals in Latin America alone by the year 2,000! One conclusion that can be drawn from these statistics is that churches grow when the power of God is released. 'Ignorance of spiritual gifts', Dr. Wagner notes, 'may be a chief cause of retarded church growth today. It also may be the root of much of the discouragement, insecurity, frustration, and guilt that plagues many Christian individuals and curtails their effectiveness for God'.[9] Pentecostals' large (and growing) numbers seem to substantiate Wagner's statement.

Over the years Pentecostalism has come under attack from both secular and Christian groups. A closer look at Pentecostal roots reveals one reason why: social differentiation. The 1906 Azusa Street revival was led by an uneducated black Holiness preacher, William J. Seymour, who attracted a poor, mostly black congregation. In my investigations of the Pentecostal healing revivalists and evangelists of the past forty years I discovered that many of the men and women come from poverty-stricken surroundings, with the associated traumas of broken homes and drug abuse. Few had much formal education. I have always wondered if racism and social snobbishness lie behind the early attacks on Pentecostals.

Pentecostal historian Vinson Synon, in his book *In the Latter Days*, outlines five fronts on which Pentecostals encountered opposition:

1 *Criticism by the press*. These attacks, from both the secular and Christian press, continue today. They usually depict Pentecostal meetings as wildly emotional, with people losing control, screaming, rolling around in the aisles, babbling like idiots – a spectacle for the world. Reports of physical healings are usually questioned in such a way as to lead readers to infer that they were staged.[10]

2 *Violent attacks*. During the first half of the century non-religious hoodlums, worked up by reports from the press, threatened or mugged Pentecostal preachers. They would disrupt meetings, burn down tents and churches, even attempting to kill them, as was the case for Oral Robers in 1947 in Tulsa, Oklahoma.[11]

3 *Criticism and rejection from holiness and fundamentalist Christians*. These Christians, with whom the Pentecostals agreed on almost every major doctrine of the faith, were their most bitter enemies. The most severe of these critics claimed that the Pentecostals were of Satan. G. Campbell Morgan called the movement 'the last vomit of Satan'.[12] (I will discuss in greater detail their theological concerns later in this chapter and in chapter nine.) In 1919, to disassociate themselves from Pentecostalism, the Pentecostal Church of the Nazarene repudiated and dropped the word 'Pentecostal' from their name, to become the Church of the Nazarene, as they are still known today. Other denominations that denounced Pentecostals included the Wesleyan church, the Church of God (Anderson, Indiana), the Salvation Army, and the Free Methodist Church. Because they were rejected by their denominations (in many cases even excommunicated), Pentecostals formed new churches.

4 *Psychological and sociological rationalisations*. While those from holiness and fundamentalist circles attacked from a theological perspective, many early twentieth-century liberals, especially university and seminary professors, used modern psychology and sociology to slander Pentecostals. Pentecostal phenomena, they said, could be explained by 'mental instability, madness, poverty, repression of the sex drive, ignorance, and lower class behaviour'.[13]

All of the early studies have been discounted, in most cases because the authors' understanding of psychology or sociology has been discredited as new theories have corrected or replaced old theories. In fact, Synon points out, later studies of Pentecostals, that compare them with control groups made up of non-tongues speakers, indicate that Pentecostals are as stable or more stable emotionally than the control group.[14]

5 *Serious theological and exegetical criticism*. Since the 1960s serious scholars, unlike earlier critics, have accepted many points of Pentecostalism. Two points that are not accepted by

most theologians are the doctrines of 'total sanctification' (which not all Pentecostals believe) and the initial evidence theory of tongues (treated more fully in the next chapter).[15] What is significant about this group of critics, Synon notes, is that they take Pentecostals seriously, accepting them as brothers and sisters.

In addition to Synon's observations, some Pentecostal revivalists (especially those not associated with any church) have been criticised because of instability in their ministries and personal lives. Their problems – all too often reported by the secular and Christian press – include mishandled finances, exaggerated claims regarding attendance at meetings and numbers and kinds of healings, and an exalted view of their ministries.

Not until 1943 in the United States, when the National Association of Evangelicals offered membership to several Pentecostal denominations, were the Pentecostals accepted by conservative evangelicals. Even then, it was not until the seventies, with the advent of the charismatic renewal, that serious dialogue and cooperation between the two groups started.

The charismatic renewal

According to David Barrett, in his massive *World Christian Encyclopedia*, over 11,000,000 people today are *practising* members of the charismatic renewal.[16] Further, a 1979 Gallup Poll commissioned by *Christianity Today* magazine, indicated that 18 percent of all US Roman Catholics over the age of eighteen in the United States *consider themselves* charismatics. In the same poll, among Lutherans, Methodists, Baptists, and Presbyterians, from 16 to 20 percent considered themselves charismatics.

The charismatic renewal differs in many respects from the Pentecostal movement. The reasons for this lie in its origins and leadership, both quite removed from Pentecostalism. I studied leaders like Dennis Bennett, Father Ralph Diorio, Father John Bertolucchi, Larry Christenson, Kevin and Dorothy Ranaghan, Ralph C. Martin, Dennis and Matthew Linn, Francis MacNutt, Father Michael Scanlan, Sister Briege McKenna, Father Edward McDonough, Agnes Sanford, Michael Harper, Michael Green, and David Watson. At the time of writing all, except

Agnes Sanford and David Watson, are alive, reflecting the youth of the movement.

Generally speaking, the leaders of the charismatic renewal are formally educated and come from stable families. They were raised in denominational churches and stayed within them, not moving out into independent-style ministries.[17]

Charismatic leaders (evangelists, healers, teachers), minister from local church bases. Many are best described as 'pastoral healers' because of their concern for pastoral follow-up to their ministry. They are usually pastors of, or are closely tied to specific congregations, though they may also travel extensively, conducting healing seminars and services. Their focus, even in their travels, is basically to members of their respective denominations. Because they maintain committed relationships and denominational loyalty, they usually have longterm success.

Finally, the charismatic leaders do not enjoy the evangelistic response among non-churched people that the Pentecostals do, because their charismatic ministries are focused in denominational churches. In fact, many members of Protestant and Catholic congregations experience personal conversion to Christ through the charismatic renewal. In this sense the renewal is thoroughly evangelistic, reaching nominal members of mainline churches. It is a renewal and reforming movement within mainline Protestant and Catholic churches – very different from Pentecostalism.

The next stage?

In 1980 I had a long, animated discussion about the charismatic renewal with David Watson. He was receiving reports that the charismatic renewal could be over, that some were even saying we were in a 'post-charismatic' era. As evidence, he mentioned the decline in conference attendance, both in the United Kingdom and the United States, frequent divisions among leaders, and (more subjectively) a general malaise marked by discouragement and discontent. It was not an encouraging report.

Yet as he spoke I thought of the large numerical increases among Pentecostals and charismatics, and wondered: Have we entered a post-charismatic era, or is the charismatic movement entering a new stage of its development? I believe a closer look at the English and American church scenes indicates the charismatic wave has not hit a breakwater. Instead, it continues to grow, no longer the institutional pariah of its early days.

Some are tempted to pronounce the charismatic renewal dead because it lacks youthful vitality. True, the early stages of the renewal are over. What we have now is a movement entering late adolescence, if not early adulthood. In order to understand this new stage in its development, we must look at what the charismatic renewal accomplished during its nascent phase.

In most denominations, the charismatic renewal has affected four areas of church life. First, the charismatic renewal has introduced new forms of worship through dance, theatre, hymnody, and (in some instances) singing in tongues. Alive, joyful music is one of the most significant contributions the charismatic movement has made to the church.

Second, the charismatic renewal has led the way in new social experiences, especially in small groups, innovative discipleship, and Christian community. (Other Christians have contributed to these efforts too, such as Keith Miller, Robert Girard, Ronald Sider, Ray Stedman, and Gene Getz.)

Third, the charismatic renewal has stimulated a revival of interest in the ministry of the Holy Spirit. In most mainline denominations, charismatic theology no longer raises the animosity it used to. To be charismatic is no longer controversial. We now find charismatic theologians among the Reformed, Lutherans, Catholics, Baptists, Presbyterians, Anglicans, and so on. In the United States, almost every mainline denomination has recognised charismatic renewal organisations, such as the Episcopal Renewal Ministries, the International Lutheran Renewal Center, the Presbyterian and Reformed Renewal Ministries, and the National Service Committee of the Catholic Charismatic Renewal. The same applies to the main denominations in Great Britain.

Finally, the charismatic movement helped renew interest in personal disciplines like prayer, Bible study, meditation, and fasting. Again, I do not imply that charismatics can take credit for all the renewed interest in these disciplines, only that they have played a significant part.

So the charismatic movement has taken root, burrowing into congregational structures, liturgy, and theology. Inevitably this has changed the renewal's character, not always for the good. There are dangers that come with acceptance, perhaps the greatest being that with respectability a loss of leavening influence is likely to occur.

Some would say the charismatic renewal is at a crossroads: will it continue to be leaven in the churches, leading the way in spirituality, or will it become moribund as many renewal movements before it? For many renewal movements of the past (especially the Catholic orders), formal recognition and acceptance by the institution have been the seeds of their weakening. This raises a difficult question, because the unity of the body of Christ demands that renewal movements work in concert with church leaders whenever possible. How can renewal movements maintain their cutting edge when they are institutionalised? Perhaps all that can be given is a stern warning: whenever renewal movements are institutionalised, they risk losing their saltiness. (Of course, the longer a movement remains outside the churches, the greater the chance for heresy or schism.)

There is another danger now facing the charismatic renewal. Acceptance by pastoral leaders does not imply permission to practise the gifts within the larger body. Many charismatics, though staying in their church denominations, have formed parachurch groups (approved by church leadership) in which they practise the charismatic gifts. Their acceptance within their denominations is circumscribed by keeping the spiritual gifts a private matter, away from the larger group. After time, though, isolation from the main body creates frustration. This often results in the loss of mainline membership to Pentecostal churches, and the death of the parachurch groups. In fact, the loss of charismatic membership is just one factor in the decline of mainline Protestant denominations. (Among Catholics, one study indicates that involvement in the charismatic renewal brings inactive Catholics back into the Church at a faster rate than involvement in the renewal encourages people to leave.[18])

I do not know what can be done to retard the modest trend of charismatics leaving mainline Protestant congregations, but denominational leaders need to consider the problem more seriously. (The charismatic members' departure is probably a subpoint under the larger problem of exodus due to theological liberalism.) Among charismatics themselves, a concerted effort to work along with their non-charismatic evangelical brothers and sisters could be one way to exert greater influence in their denominations, as well as receive encouragement and support. Of course, non-charismatic evangelicals must be willing to cooperate in this effort, something they have not always been eager to do.

The evangelical key

One obstacle to greater evangelical unity has been labels: who are the evangelicals and what are their subgroups? Evangelicals are a diverse group. Quoting from Michael Cassidy, 'The term evangelical describes the broad spectrum of Christians who limit religious authority to the Bible and who stress the New Testament doctrines of conversion, new birth, and justification by grace through faith alone. Evangelicals hold to the full inspiration of the Bible as the Word of God'.[19] Under this broad definition, evangelicals include Pentecostals, charismatics, fundamentalists, and conservative evangelicals. We are sprinkled throughout mainline churches, concentrated in Pentecostal denominations and smaller, conservative evangelical denominations and independent Bible congregations.

By *conservative evangelicals* I mean a subgrouping within evangelicalism that is non-charismatic but not necessarily anti-charismatic. Charismatics and conservative evangelicals hold every major point of the Christian faith in common. Conservative evangelicals aggressively refute the influences of theological liberalism. Mainline liberals, not understanding the nuances of conservative evangelicals, often throw them together with their less-tolerant fundamentalist cousins.[20] But this is a mistake, because conservative evangelicals as a group are more open to new ideas and relationships than are fundamentalists.

I believe a key element in the next stage of the charismatic renewal, one that already appears to be taking place, could be the coming together of these conservative evangelicals with charismatics and Pentecostals. This unity could do much for both groups. For charismatics, conservative evangelicals offer a rich theological heritage and concern for personal evangelism and missions. For conservative evangelicals, charismatics offer spiritual renewal, a deeper experience of God's working directly in their lives.

Theology is *very* important in one way or another for conservative evangelicals. Therein lies an obstacle as we attempt to understand signs and wonders: part of the conservative evangelicals' theological heritage denies that the gifts function today.

So a major question that must be addressed to further conservative evangelical-charismatic unity is a theological one: the cessation theory of the charismatic gifts. The most popular conservative-evangelical cessation theory is based on an interpretation of 1 Corinthians 13:10 '. . . but when *perfection* comes, the imperfect disappears'. Conservative evangelicals teach that 'perfection' in the verse refers to the completed canon of scripture (the New Testament) – recognised at the Council of Carthage in 397 – and 'the imperfect' refers to the charismatic gifts, which have now 'disappeared' or ceased. (I introduced this argument earlier in chapter seven.)

Referring to the supernatural gifts, one author writes, 'These [miracles, healings, tongues, and interpretation of tongues] were certain enablements given to certain believers for the purpose of authenticating or confirming God's word when it was proclaimed in the early church before the scriptures were penned. These sign gifts were temporary . . . once the Word of God was inscriptured, the sign gifts were no longer needed and they ceased'.[21]

The argument for equating 'perfection' with the closing of the New Testament canon has two parts:

1 The word 'perfection' is a neuter noun, and must, they imply, refer to a thing, not a person. Since scripture is a thing and is neuter in gender, it follows that the Bible is the 'perfect' thing to which Paul is referring.

2 This interpretation, they assert, fits well with verses 8, 9, 11, and 12 of the same passage in 1 Corinthians 13: '. . . where there are tongues, they will be stilled . . . When I was a child, I talked like a child . . . Now I know in part; then I shall know fully, even as I am fully known'. In this line of reasoning, tongues are childish, while scripture is mature.

There are several weaknesses with this interpretation, not the least of which is that a major doctrine is being built on a fairly unclear passage. Where else in scripture is there a hint of this teaching?

Beyond this, while 'perfection' is a neuter noun, in Greek there is no warrant for limiting its reference to another neuter noun. A neuter noun or pronoun can be used to describe masculine and (or) feminine things or persons. One example is the Greek word translated 'begotten' (*monogenes*), found in John 3:16. Begotten is a neuter noun used in reference to men and women, in this case to Christ. The word 'Spirit' (*pneuma*) is also a neuter noun, and scripture is clear that the Spirit is not a thing – he is the third person of the Trinity.

Perhaps a bigger problem is that the interpretation calls for the leaving of the immediate context of 1 Corinthians 13 in order to determine the identity of 'perfection'. A jump to 2 Timothy 3:15–16 is made, where 'scripture' is neuter. This is an arbitrary jump.

F. F. Bruce offers a more plausible interpretation of what 'perfection' refers to: the second coming of Christ. This interpretation appears to fit well within the overall context of 1 Corinthians 1:7, 'Therefore you do not lack any spiritual gift as you eagerly wait for our Lord Jesus Christ to be revealed'.[22]

It would be a mistake to think that theology is the only obstacle to conservative evangelical and charismatic unity. In fact, I have discovered that attempts to unify around theology are unsatisfying. Fear, for example, is another barrier. In particular there is the fear that the authority of scripture will be undermined by gifts like prophecy and tongues, that subjective experience will replace objective truth as the plumb line of Christianity.

There is also a cultural barrier. Although not consciously understood, conservative evangelicals in recent years have moved up in social, economic, and educational status, making it harder to relate to Pentecostals.[23] Pentecostals have also been moving up the social scale, though not as rapidly as the conservative evangelicals. On the other hand, many conservative evangelicals have been favourably affected by the charismatic renewal (by people of similar social standing to themselves), even when, due to theological reservations, they have not experienced the gifts.

Perhaps the next stage of the Holy Spirit, one affecting conservative evangelicals, will come with different models of how the charismatic gifts should function, such as in power evangelism. Just as Pentecostalism and the charismatic renewal have produced different results as they affect different groups of people, this next stage of the charismatic renewal will have a different flavour, with a particular emphasis on personal evangelism. C. Peter Wagner reflects this thinking when asked if he considers himself a charismatic or Pentecostal:

> I see myself as neither a charismatic nor a Pentecostal. I belong to Lake Avenue Congregational Church. I'm a Congregationalist. My church is not a charismatic church, although some of our members are charismatic.
>
> However, our church is more and more open to the same way that the Holy Spirit does work among charismatics. For example, our pastor gives an invitation after every service for people who need physical healing and inner healing to come forward and go to the prayer room and be anointed with oil and prayed for, and we have teams of people who know how to pray for the sick.
>
> We like to think that we are doing it in a Congregational way; we're not doing it in a charismatic way. But we're getting the same results.[24]

Conservative evangelicals frequently ask me questions about 'the baptism of the Holy Spirit', a hallmark of Pentecostalism and the charismatic renewal. Is the term biblical? Does everyone have to speak in tongues? And what about the teaching that we do not have the Holy Spirit until we speak in tongues? How is the Pentecostal experience of the Holy Spirit related to conservative-evangelical teaching on being filled with the Spirit? Answers to these questions are the topics of the next chapter.

9

EMPOWERED BY THE HOLY SPIRIT

In the summer of 1967 a friend of mine, Scott, attended a students' retreat at Arrowhead Springs, California, the headquarters of Campus Crusade for Christ International. A nineteen year old UCLA student, he had been a committed Christian for five years.

Scott's spiritual life had recently stalled. He was looking for more from God, something to empower his life and give clearer purpose.

Arrowhead Springs is carved into the mountains overlooking the city of San Bernardino. During an earlier era, it was an old health spa frequented by Hollywood stars; Greta Garbo and Clark Gable were reported to have sought 'the cure' in sulphur-laced, steamy caverns deep below the main hotel. Perhaps, Scott thought, he would find a spiritual cure during this weeklong conference.

On arriving he discovered that he was to sleep in the hotel basement on a makeshift cot. Over 700 students from the United States and Canada jammed the facilities; it was not to be a Hollywood holiday. But that suited him well. It created an atmosphere of excitement and expectant faith: if these students came from hundreds and even thousands of miles away surely God would show up!

The theme of the conference was personal evangelism. Towards the end of the week the students were to be transported on buses to local beaches where, going two-by-two, they would put into action what they had been taught: the evangelising of complete strangers.

Scott was apprehensive about going out, especially since he had been raised on the beaches of southern California and was fearful of embarrassing encounters with old surfing buddies. Also, the idea of confronting complete strangers with a planned presentation became more frightening as the week progressed. At least, he soon discovered, they were not going to his home beach.

The evening before they went out, Dr. William Bright, president of Campus Crusade, presented a teaching about the Holy Spirit. His points were very simple: we cannot successfully live the Christian life in our own strength; the Father has sent the Holy Spirit to empower us; we are commanded in scripture to 'be filled with the Holy Spirit'.

For years Scott had been taught not to focus on the Holy Spirit, lest he weaken his relationship with Christ, or fall into the excesses of the Pentecostals. This could be dangerous, leading possibly to deceit by the Devil, even speaking in tongues. Besides, he heard many times, our primary purpose should be fulfilling the great commission. An emphasis on the Holy Spirit might detract us from this important task.

But Dr. Bright's talk stirred Scott deeply, allaying many of his fears. Dr. Bright said that only through the power of the Holy Spirit could we fulfil the great commission. (It was one of the few positive teachings Scott had ever heard on the third person of the Trinity.) 'Perhaps,' Scott mused, 'this is the key to the refreshing I seek'.

That night Scott could hardly sleep, intermittently awakening thinking about Dr. Bright's words. By one o'clock he was wide-eyed, staring at the tangle of pipes and electrical tubing overhead, sensing God calling him to open his heart fully to the Holy Spirit. So he slipped out of bed, dressed, and found a quiet place under a lonely palm tree in the hotel grounds.

Unsure of what to expect, his hunger for God motivated him to pray. 'Holy Spirit', he pleaded, 'I have been living in my own strength too long. Now I yield every part of my life to you. Come and fill me'.

What happened next was outside of anything Scott had been taught about how God works. First, he felt a rush of power come over his body, a warm, tingling feeling as he never had before experienced. With that rush came a peace and urging to worship God. As he began worshipping he was soon speaking in tongues – though initially he was unsure of what it was. After praying and

worshipping for an hour he opened his Bible and began reading
. . . and reading . . . and reading – late into the night. Scripture
came alive, the very word of God leaping off the pages.

The next day, knowing staff members were not sympathetic to
charismatic phenomena, he told no one of his experience. Was it
real? he wondered. It had to be. He was a different person,
though confused about the meaning of what happened. As the
time to go to the beaches approached, he noticed the gospel
burned in his heart, pressing every part of his being with an
urgency to tell others about Jesus Christ.

Scott boarded the bus without any fear, though still not
looking forward to talking with strangers. But now he sensed his
experience the night before would help him on the beaches.

His partner, Jim, a student at the University of North Caroli-
na, was apprehensive. Scott knew that the Holy Spirit was telling
him to take the lead on the beach. He quietly prayed as the bus
snaked its way across the freeways leading to Newport Beach.

Newport Beach is typical of many beaches in southern California – sand covered with thousands of young people flocked
around blasting radios, sharing the latest gossip, telling jokes,
and watching other boys and girls walk by. Out into this mass of
oily, tanning flesh went the God squads.

Scott and Jim first approached two Hispanic teenage boys,
asking if they would mind participating in a religious survey (the
survey was part of the evangelism programme, a way of beginning conversation with strangers). Soon they were talking about
Jesus Christ. Two girls joined the conversation, then another
three boys. Scott had quickly put the Four Spiritual Laws aside
and was telling the teenagers about their sins and God's grace.
As he spoke he received insights about the teenagers – sexual
sins, problems with parents, problems at school – that were right
on target. Supernaturally knowing what their greatest needs
were, he spoke about God's love and righteousness in a way that
opened their hearts. Jim stood by, astonished.

Within thirty minutes several of the teenagers were weeping,
falling to their knees, repenting from their sin and turning to
Christ. Before the day was over at least a dozen young people
made Christian commitments. In several instances students who
initially joined the conversation only to mock and ridicule Scott
ended on their faces, weeping, trembling, repenting.

Whatever term one applies to what happened to Scott when he was overwhelmed by the Holy Spirit under the palm tree – filled, baptised, empowered – the result was power evangelism. Sometimes, though, terminology is misleading and confusing. This discourages Christians from experiencing God's power in the way Scott did that night at Arrowhead Springs.

Coming to terms

Andrew Murray, a nineteenth century evangelical pastor and writer, wrote in his book, *The Believer's Full Blessing of Pentecost*, 'The greatest need of the church, and the thing which, above all others, believers ought to seek for with one mind and with their whole heart, is to be filled with the Spirit of God . . . Every day ought to be a Pentecostal season in the church of Christ'.[1] For many Christians (as was true for Scott and me) some of the greatest obstacles to a daily Pentecost are questions surrounding the pentecostal doctrine of 'the baptism in (or of) the Holy Spirit'.

The concept of being baptised in the Holy Spirit is a controversial doctrine. The term being found in scripture, over the past 150 years Christians have understood its meaning in a variety of ways, almost always causing great misunderstanding and division among themselves.

Satan has been particularly effective in stirring up controversy over the Holy Spirit. Commenting on this problem, A. W. Tozer has written:

Satan has opposed the doctrine of the Spirit-filled life about as bitterly as any doctrine there is. He has confused it, opposed it, surrounded it with false notions and fears. He has blocked every effort of the Church of Christ to receive from the Father her divine and blood-bought patrimony. The church has tragically neglected this great liberating truth – that there is now for the child of God a full and wonderful and completely satisfying anointing with the Holy Spirit. The Spirit-filled life is not a special, deluxe edition of Christianity. It is part and parcel of the total plan of God for His people.[2]

In the nineteenth century, Methodists frequently used 'baptism in the Holy Spirit' to refer to a post-conversion experience, a 'second blessing'. In the eighteenth century John Wesley defined the second blessing as 'entire sanctification'. By this Wesley thought Christians could be perfected – the sinful nature eradicated – through a special second anointing of the Holy Spirit.[3] This is the hallmark doctrine of Wesleyan and holiness teaching, though only holiness Pentecostals today refer to it as the baptism of the Holy Spirit.[4]

By the turn of the century, the terms 'baptism in the Holy Spirit' and 'pentecostal' were popular among evangelicals outside of holiness circles. The baptism of the Holy Spirit was particularly emphasised in the writings of A. J. Gordon (the father of Gordon College), F. B. Meyer, A. B. Simpson (the founder of the Christian and Missionary Alliance denomination), Andrew Murray, R. A. Torrey (the first president of Moody Bible Institute, Chicago), and evangelist Dwight L. Moody. This is how Moody described his baptism in the Holy Spirit:

I began to cry as never before, for a greater blessing from God. The hunger increased; I really felt that I did not want to live any longer. [He had been a Christian, and not only a Christian but a minister, and in charge of a Mission for some time; he was getting conversions, but still he wanted more.] I kept on crying all the time that God would fill me with his Spirit. Well, one day in the city of New York – oh! what a day, I cannot describe it, I seldom refer to it. It is almost too sacred an experience to name. Paul had an experience of which he never spoke for 14 years. I can only say, God revealed himself to me, and I had such an experience of his love that I had to ask him to stay his hand.

Commenting on Moody's experience, D. Martyn Lloyd-Jones writes: 'It was so overwhelming, he felt as if he was going to be physically crushed. The love of God! That is what is meant by "the love of God in your hearts". That is the baptism of the Spirit. That is what turned D. L. Moody from a good, regular, ordinary minister, into the evangelist who was so signally used of God in this and in other countries.'[5]

Through these authors, a significant shift occurred in the understanding of the purpose of the Spirit's baptism. Along with

Wesley's 'entire sanctification', a second understanding arose with a new emphasis on the anointing of the Holy Spirit for witness and service. (This created a conflict with those who held the Wesleyan holiness doctrine.)

The new emphasis was spread through Keswick 'Higher Life' conferences in England and their American counterpart in Massachusetts, the Northfield Conferences, conducted by evangelist D. L. Moody. R. A. Torrey summarises their teaching:

> The baptism with the Holy Spirit is an operation of the Holy Spirit distinct from and subsequent from his regenerating work . . . an impartation of power for service. [This baptism was] not merely for the apostles, not merely for those of the apostolic age, but for 'all that are afar off; even as many as the Lord our God shall call' . . . it is for every believer in every age of the church's history.[6]

While the late nineteenth century holiness and Keswick movements taught on the need of a baptism of the Holy Spirit for sanctification or empowering for service, they did not recognise the experience of charismatic gifts in such a baptism. But R. A. Torrey, writing in 1895, wondered about this:

> In my early study of the baptism with the Holy Spirit I noticed that in many instances those who were so baptised 'spoke in tongues,' and the question often came into my mind, if one is baptised with the Holy Spirit will he not speak with tongues? But I saw no one so speaking and I often wondered, is there any one today who actually is baptised with the Holy Spirit?[7]

At this time the gift of tongues was rarely experienced, which explains Torrey's perplexed comment. But, as Pentecostal historian Vinson Synon has noted, 'shouting, "dancing in the spirit", falling out "under the power", or catching the "holy laugh"' were frequent phenomena at holiness gatherings.[8]

Division

Understood against the background of nineteenth century holiness and Keswick history (as well as parallel trends among Roman Catholics[9]), the early twentieth century Pentecostal movement is not surprising. Beginning in 1901 at Charles Parham's Bethel Bible School in Topeka, Kansas, and the 1906 Azusa Street revival in Los Angeles, California, under William J. Seymour's leadership, large numbers of people spoke in tongues when prayed over for 'the baptism in the Holy Spirit'. There were other phenomena as well, including expulsions of evil spirits, words of knowledge, healings, and prophecy.

Pentecostalism was born, and with it yet another understanding of the term 'baptism in the Holy Spirit'. Soon the Pentecostals were teaching that through experiencing 'the baptism of the Holy Spirit' Christians receive the third person of the Trinity. Further, it was thought that the initial evidence of receiving the Holy Spirit is speaking in tongues.

Pentecostals were and are divided on interpreting whether this experience is equated with Wesley's 'entire sanctification' or Moody's 'empowering for service'.[10] For example, members of the Pentecostal Holiness Church fall within the former category, the Assemblies of God in the latter.

The development of early twentieth century Pentecostalism forced conservative evangelicals, who at that time frequently used the term 'baptism in the Holy Spirit', to consider the charismatic gifts. By and large, those from both the holiness and Keswick traditions rejected the charismatic gifts. The conservative evangelicals claimed that the gifts ceased in the early church, that Pentecostalism was a serious error, perhaps even demonic. Conservative evangelicals were especially offended by the teaching that tongues are the evidence of the baptism of the Holy Spirit, and that those who have not spoken in tongues do not have the Holy Spirit.

In order to disassociate themselves from the Pentecostals, the term 'baptism in the Holy Spirit' fell into disfavour among conservative evangelicals. Instead, they used the term 'filling' to describe believers' initiatory (and ongoing) experience of the Holy Spirit. As the Pentecostals continued to attract more people, many conservative evangelicals reacted, becoming more entrenched in their criticisms of Pentecostal doctrine. In many instances, to protect their people from what they considered serious error or excess of the Pentecostals, conservative evangelical pastors discouraged their people from seeking any experience with the Holy Spirit.

At the same time dispensationalism, popularised through the Scofield Bible and the many pastors coming out of newly formed seminaries and Bible colleges, was growing in influence. Of all theologies, dispensationalism is probably the most antagonistic towards the charismatic gifts and Pentecostalism.

Only in the past fifteen years have conservative evangelicals and Pentecostals begun serious dialogue regarding their differences over the Holy Spirit. Perhaps the key question (though by no means the only question) for both groups concerns the theological basis for our experience of the Holy Spirit. Conservative evangelicals have always taught that we should first establish the theological basis for activity, then explore the experience. As Pentecostalism and the charismatic renewal have grown, evangelicals have renewed their interest in the Holy Spirit, in many instances changing negative attitudes towards the charismatic gifts. At the same time, Pentecostal theologians, perhaps through the influence of the charismatic renewal, are attempting more indepth biblical reflection on the meaning of the baptism of the Holy Spirit. Both groups realise that any resolution of the conflict is to be found in scripture.

One baptism, many fillings

The concept of being baptised in the Holy Spirit originated with John the Baptist: 'I baptise you with water. But one more powerful than I will come, the thongs of whose sandals I am not worthy to untie. *He will baptise you with the Holy Spirit* and with fire' (Luke 3:16). Later, at Christ's baptism, John proclaimed, '. . . the one who sent me to baptise with water told me, "The man on whom you see the Spirit come down and remain is *he who will baptise with the Holy Spirit*." I have seen and I testify that this [Jesus] is the Son of God' (John 1:33–34).

From John's teaching we learn:
1 John taught that Israel should expect a new baptism with the coming of the Messiah.[11]
2 John contrasted his baptism with the Messiah's, which would come at a future, undisclosed time.
3 John's baptism was with water, the Messiah's would be with the Holy Spirit.

In a post-resurrection appearance, Jesus reminded the dis-

ciples of what John taught when he said, 'John baptised with
water, but in a few days you will be baptised with the Holy Spirit'
(Acts 1:5). A few days later, at Pentecost, they were baptised
with the Holy Spirit.

In explaining to his fellow apostles how the gift of the Holy
Spirit was poured out on the Gentiles (something the apostles
found difficult to accept), Peter said: 'I remembered what the
Lord had said, "John baptised with water, but you will be
baptised with the Holy Spirit." So if God gave them the same gift
as he gave us, who believed in the Lord Jesus Christ, who was I to
think that I could oppose God!' (Acts 11:16, 17).

The phrase employing the noun form for baptism – '*the
baptism* of the Holy Spirit' – is not found in the New Testament.
The verb form – '*being baptised* in the Holy Spirit' – is almost
always used, with the lone exception being the words of Paul
found in Acts 19:3 – 'What baptism did you receive?' But while
the phrase 'the baptism of the Holy Spirit' is not employed, the
phenomenon John predicted, which Christ said to expect, and
which occurs throughout Acts needs to be called by some name.

The English word 'baptise' is transliterated from the Greek
baptizo, which means to dip or immerse. It conveys the sense of
being overwhelmed. John the Baptist, Jesus, and Peter all taught
that we should seek to be overwhelmed by the Spirit.

More confusing is that in the book of Acts, being baptised in
the Holy Spirit is equated with being 'filled' with the Holy Spirit.
'All of them', Luke says in Acts 2:4 'were *filled* with the Holy
Spirit and began to speak in other tongues as the Spirit enabled'.
This may be one reason why conservative evangelicals are more
comfortable describing the ongoing Christian experience of the
Holy Spirit as a filling rather than a baptism.

I have discovered that the argument concerning the baptism of
the Spirit usually comes down to a question of labels. Good
medicine may be incorrectly labelled, which is probably true in
this case. The Pentecostal experience of God is better than their
explanation of it. Unfortunately, the reverse can be true. It is
possible to affirm orthodox theology, yet have little Christian
character, service, and experience. An accurate label may adorn
any empty bottle.

Terms like 'Trinity' and 'receiving Christ as Saviour' are not
found in the New Testament either, yet few object to their use.

Whether called baptism or filling, God's gifts and power are essential for witness and service. All Christians are commanded to seek the Holy Spirit (see Ephesians 5:18), regardless of how that experience is labelled.

Still, the question remains, what is the best term to describe what John predicted and which then occurred in Acts?

Charles Hummel, in *Fire in the Fireplace*, points out that Paul and Luke used the term 'baptism in the Holy Spirit' differently. Paul used it to mean an initial action of the Holy Spirit that incorporates the individual into the body of Christ at conversion (especially see 1 Corinthians 12:13). Luke used it to mean an endowment with power for effective witness and service, an experience that can be repeated.[12]

Clark Pinnock, commenting on the difference between Paul and Luke, notes:

> Baptism is a flexible metaphor, not a technical term. Luke seems to regard it as synonymous with 'fulness' (Acts 2:4; cf. 11:16). Therefore, so long as we recognise conversion as truly a baptism in the Spirit, there is no reason why we cannot use 'baptism' to refer to subsequent fillings of the Spirit as well. This latter experience, or experiences, should not be tied in with the tight 'second blessing' schema, but should be seen as an actualisation of what we have already received in the initial charismatic experience, which is conversion.[13]

Following this line of reasoning, which most conservative evangelicals agree with, the born-again experience is the consummate charismatic experience – what Paul would refer to as being baptised in the Holy Spirit. Any ensuing interaction between the individual and the Holy Spirit would come under the heading of 'fillings', as taught by Paul. Further, these fillings may happen again and again – they are both initiatory and repeatable.

So, following Paul, it is probably best to speak of 'being filled with the Holy Spirit'. But in Luke we find warrant in using 'being baptised with the Holy Spirit'. Both terms convey the urgency for Christians to seek sincerely the power of the Holy Spirit.

Timing

When does our baptism or filling occur? As Pinnock commented, the filling is both initiatory (John 3:3–6) and repeatable (Galatians 5:25). The Spirit's coming on the disciples at Pentecost anointed them to establish the church. Repeated fillings empowered them for prophecy, healing, apostleship, and so on. In the book of Acts, Peter was filled with the Holy Spirit twice (2:4 and 4:31).

As we have need, God provides his Counsellor (John 14:16, 26; 16:7, 13–15). Throughout the book of Acts, 'Luke takes his subjects where he finds them and leaves them in a fully Spirit-baptised state, which is the same as to say they became true believers'.[14] There is no identifiable pattern or 'correct' sequence for being filled with the Spirit. 'Completeness', theologian Russell Spittler notes, 'and not subsequence, strikes me as a better category by which to understand the arrival of the Spirit in Acts'.[15] Our concern therefore, should not be *when* we experience the Spirit's filling but *that* we experience it.

I believe that when a person is converted he receives the Holy Spirit. He may or may not experience the Holy Spirit at that time. Conversion and the initial filling experience of the Holy Spirit can happen simultaneously. Certainly the potential for that is there. In fact, I now frequently see people receive Christ and get filled with the Holy Spirit at the same time. Why? I teach that because the Holy Spirit is now in them, they may by faith, actualise his power and gifts.

Anyone born again has the potential of experiencing the power and gifts of the Holy Spirit. We should expect this experience – scripture teaches it is a part of the normal Christian life. If the experience of the Holy Spirit is not preached or seen by Christians – which is true of many evangelical churches – they will not expect these things to happen, and they will not happen. 'Faith comes from hearing the message, and the message is heard through the word of Christ' (Romans 10:17). As Christians learn and see that there is more to experience, they are willing to take a chance, step out in faith, and receive God's power.

When I talk with evangelicals about the Holy Spirit, I ask if when they were born again they received the Spirit. If they answer yes (and they should), I tell them all that remains is to *actualise* that which the Spirit has, all that is required is to release the gifts. I then lay hands on them and say, 'Be filled with the Spirit' – and they are.

I have discovered that when Pentecostals say Christians need 'to receive the Holy Spirit', they do not necessarily mean that believers do not have the Holy Spirit before being baptised in the Holy Spirit. The lack of precision in their language is unfortunate, contributing to misunderstanding about what they teach. Dennis Bennett, in *Nine O'Clock in the Morning*, clarifies the concept: 'Receiving the Holy Spirit or being "baptised in the Holy Spirit" does not mean getting the Holy Spirit, but "receiving" or "making welcome", permitting the Holy Spirit to fill more areas of our lives and to flow out from us to the world'.

Tongues for everyone?

Another controversial question regarding the Holy Spirit involves tongues: May one be filled or baptised in the Holy Spirit without speaking in tongues? That question has always divided Pentecostals and conservative evangelicals.[16] Pentecostal theologian Russell Spittler responds:

> As I see it, the Bible gives no direct answer to this question for the reason that nowhere in scripture is the question directly raised . . . Luke's concern in Acts, it seems to me, is not to show that speaking in tongues is 'initial physical evidence' of the baptism in the Holy Spirit . . . It is not so much 'tongues is the evidence of the Spirit' as it is that 'the Spirit is the evidence of being a Christian.'[17]

Speaking in tongues as an evidence of baptism or filling is not mentioned in the epistles. It is from the book of Acts that Pentecostals base their teaching on the necessity of tongues as evidence of the Spirit's baptism (see 2:4; 10:46; 19:6). Yet there are many instances in Acts where Luke mentions nothing about tongues speaking as a result of being baptised in the Spirit (see 4:23–31; 8:14–39; 9:1–42; 17:32–34).

Russell Spittler further states that 'there are thoroughly charismatic churches where glossolalia [tongues] is not viewed as the necessary initial physical evidence of Spirit-baptism. The one who finds himself called to glossolalic levels of encounter with the Holy Spirit by no means is necessarily committed to the theological hardware of the classical Pentecostal churches. The Spirit still blows where he wills'.[18]

Yet while tongues are not the focus of the Spirit's filling, spiritual gifts cannot be avoided. Too many evangelicals want the Spirit but not the gifts, an attitude that violates scriptural teaching: 'But eagerly desire the greater gifts' (1 Corinthians 12:31).

Social barriers

Unfortunately, legitimate theological questions are not the only obstacles that must be overcome by conservative evangelicals. Social barriers are frequently greater than theological barriers. Conservative evangelicals are exposed to many immature Christians who practise the charismatic gifts, persons not formed in mature character. What put me off for years as a pastor was the steady stream of people coming to me after having been baptised in the Holy Spirit, people who were now operating with an elitist attitude, telling me that I was not as spiritual as they were. Of course, I measured them on the basis of their family life and character – what I think are sound bases for judging growth and maturity of individuals – and I often saw very immature people.

But this was a false basis for judging the validity of spiritual gifts, because the gifts are not given only to *mature* people, they are given to *willing* people. This is not to denigrate the importance of Christian character in the right functioning of the gifts; but we must not confuse immaturity in the exercise of gifts with the authenticity of the gifts themselves. It took several years for me to realise that these people had become barriers rather than bridges to my experiencing and understanding the Holy Spirit. When I came to Fuller Seminary I became aware that some of my colleagues spoke in tongues. I recognised in them mature character and lifestyle.

That Fuller Seminary, the largest evangelical seminary in the world, has Pentecostals on faculty demonstrates greater understanding between conservative evangelicals and Pentecostals today. Pentecostals are beginning to take conservative evangelical concerns more seriously, grappling with tough theological questions, not despising serious theological study as they did earlier in this century. In this regard, the new David du Plessis Centre for Christian Spirituality at Fuller Seminary is heartening.

On the part of conservative evangelicals there is change too; strident anti-Pentecostalism, so common only twenty years ago, is receding. Symbolic of this change is Campus Crusade for Christ's recent announcement of change in hiring policy: they now allow Christians who speak in tongues on staff, though they are still not allowed to practise charismatic gifts around other staff members or students. Nevertheless, this is a significant change. Had my friend Scott, whom I wrote about at the beginning of this chapter, been filled with the Holy Spirit today rather than in 1967, Campus Crusade leaders would have affirmed his experience, perhaps resulting in a greater evangelistic harvest. At least, he might not have remained confused for years about how, as an evangelical, the spiritual gifts operate.

Still, whether conservative evangelical or Pentecostal, the Spirit of Christ, who dwells in us, desires to express himself through us. It is not enough to acknowledge a theological basis for the practice of the gifts but prefer that no one actually practises them. (To resist the gifts is to resist Christ. This is not only a conservative evangelical problem: a 1979 *Christianity Today*-Gallup Poll indicates that only seventeen percent of all claiming to be Pentecostals or charismatics in America spoke in tongues, indicating a discrepancy between their belief and practice.)

Tongues, prophecy, words of knowledge – many such experiences I have described in this book – are an assault on Western Christians' predilection towards personal control of their experience. We find security in the predictable, intellectually understandable experience. In this regard, the Holy Spirit is outside of our control: signs and wonders defy the logic of a scientific worldview.

There is a sense in which we do control the Holy Spirit. We can always choose to shut him out, to turn away from his leading, to reserve areas of our life for our own control. But as we do, these choices affect the very root of our humanity. C. S. Lewis describes how our choices affect us in this way:

> I would say that every time you make a choice you are turning the central part of you, the part of you that chooses,

into something a little different from what it was before. And taking your life as a whole, with all your innumerable choices, all your life long you are slowly turning this central thing either into a heavenly creature or into a hellish creature: either into a creature that is in harmony with God, and with other creatures, and with itself, or else into one that is in a state of war and hatred with God, and with its fellow-creatures, and with itself.[19]

As Christians, the most fundamental choice that we make is to submit our lives to the control of the Holy Spirit, to ask him to actualise all that he has for us, to release the gifts. If you have never taken this step of faith, you may be filled with the Spirit right now. All that is required is your cooperation in opening your heart to God, asking the Spirit to fill you and take control of your life.

10

'WHAT SHALL I DO?'

In 1981 I was invited to preach at St Andrew's Anglican Church in Chorleywood, Herts, England. David Watson and Eddie Gibbs had encouraged Bishop David Pytches, vicar of St. Andrew's, to invite me to speak. He consented, inviting me for two days, from Saturday morning to Sunday evening.

St. Andrew's is a suburban church composed mostly of professionals, including members of the House of Commons, doctors, lawyers and educators. The pastor before David Pytches had introduced St. Andrew's to the charismatic renewal, which most of the members received, though in a fairly subdued fashion. St. Andrew's was and is a 'properly Anglican' congregation; I was apprehensive about how the people would respond to teaching about signs and wonders.

Saturday morning I taught about church growth, introducing them to the relationship between the miraculous and growing churches. That evening I spoke on healing, seeing only a moderate response when I prayed over people at the end of the session.

By Sunday morning the church was buzzing about the power of God, some of the people being upset with what I said and did the previous evening. After the eucharist liturgy, I and my associates again prayed over people. My brother-in-law, Bob Fulton, prayed over a woman who was blind in one eye. When she told Bob what her problem was, he heard her incorrectly, thinking that she had said, 'I have arthritis.' So he prayed for her to be healed of arthritis (which she didn't have), resulting in her receiving sight. Her response was to begin yelping – something not well received by many in the congregation. Bob almost fainted. By Sunday afternoon David Pytches' phone was ringing constantly with people calling to express concern about what they thought were excesses.

That evening I became concerned about how the congregation was receiving what I had said. But when the evening service began I sensed the powerful presence of the Holy Spirit. Before we left many people were healed and, so it was later reported to me, as many as 100 young people gave their lives over to God that evening or immediately after. Many of them are today preparing for the ministry. To that date, it was the most powerful meeting outside of Vineyard Christian Fellowship gatherings that I had conducted.

David Pytches' response throughout the weekend was joy and laughter – although neither he nor I fully understood what God was doing. As I left on Monday morning, his last words, spoken in a mocking dismay, were 'You've torn my church into bits and pieces. What shall I do?'

'What shall I do?' How many times I have heard that question after people have experienced the kingdom of God, tasting the Holy Spirit. When I finish teaching the last session of the course The Miraculous and Church Growth at Fuller Seminary, I am often approached by students asking how what I have taught is meant to work in their churches. Over half of my students are pastors or missionaries home on furlough, so for them, like David Pytches, this is a pressing concern.

Go home and be one

Several years ago a Methodist pastor who had recently taken the signs and wonders course at Fuller Seminary wrote to me asking for advice. On the verge of retirement, he had initially enrolled in the course to gain credits that would improve his denominational pension. But by the end of the term his life was changed – he had been empowered with the Holy Spirit, radically changing his outlook towards the ministry.

'John,' he wrote, 'I serve on countless committees and do an endless amount of administration. I want to minister in the power of God, but how can I if I'm always going to district meetings, financial committees, and other sorts of bureaucratic gatherings?'

My advice to him was simple: it does not matter where you are but what you are. Like Jesus, we are called to do the Father's bidding wherever he has placed us. Instead of looking to change things outwardly, I cautioned him, we should let God change us inwardly.

Later I heard back from him. 'John,' he wrote, 'I took your advice. Now I go to committee meetings and ask God to lead me to meet people's needs, to show me what he wants me to say and do. Rarely does a session go by where I do not pray over another pastoral leader or committee member. Further, wherever I go I am always asking the Father to show me his will so I can do his works.'

The pastor explained how he would ask folks, 'How are you?' and when they told him their problems, he prayed over them, with excellent results. He did not go into a long explanation with the people about what he was doing, he simply did it.

This is the way most of the members of the Vineyard Christian Fellowship go about their daily lives. One member of our church, Keith Endow, is an estate agent who regularly prays over clients who have needs. And they never complain, because the Holy Spirit always comes on them. For example, recently he was showing a client through the home of an elderly couple who were moving due to the recent divorce of a daughter. All around their home were photographs and paintings of their daughter, son-in-law, and grandchildren. The couple were moving to help their daughter through a difficult time. So, just before leaving, Keith told them he was a Christian and asked if he could pray for them. They readily accepted, the Holy Spirit bringing a peace and blessing to them.

It is important that we are where God wants us to be. Yet I am convinced that Christians frequently use their situation in life as an excuse for not being used by God right now, that they too often think if only they were in the 'right place' they could do the types of things I have described in this book.

Disciples of Jesus first

Another question people frequently ask is 'Under whom can I get discipled in power evangelism? Who will teach me how to do it?'

I do not discount the need for practical discipleship, the need to learn from older and more experienced brothers and sisters in all areas of Christian living. But when I hear people asking this question, sometimes I wonder if they are bypassing the only true discipler: Jesus. He made the first disciples, and he has continued to make disciples down through the centuries. But too often we allow men to take his place, missing out on the opportunity to receive his lordship in our hearts.

We should read good Christian literature, go to conferences, and learn from those who are effective at what I have described in this book. But we should beware of allowing men to take the place of God.

Waiting on God

Finally, we must learn to wait on God, allowing him to speak, act, lead – always yielding our right to control whatever situation we are in. There is something very simple, almost childlike, about power evangelism. God gives impressions, and we act on them. If he does not speak to us, then we wait – something difficult for action-orientated Western people to do.

This is a simple faith, the kind that Jesus cultivated in the disciples: he always looked for responsive people, men and women who acted on his words, even when they did not understand the words' ramifications (which was often the case). 'Come, follow me' was all it took for most of the disciples to leave everything behind and follow the kingdom of God. Our call is no different today.

When the cloud-burst of the Holy Spirit came on them at Pentecost, when drenched with his power, the key to the disciples' success remained the same: emptying themselves from all desire to control God, yielding their lives in service to him.

What should we do? David Pytches stayed at St. Andrew's, not creating radical organisational changes, but encouraging the people to open their hearts to God, walk in his power, and obey his voice. He watched St. Andrew's become a greater source of spiritual renewal and evangelism in the United Kingdom. Others might be homemakers, factory workers, secretaries, sales-persons, teachers. But we all face the same challenge as David Pytches and the people of St. Andrew's: to yield control of our lives to the Holy Spirit, learning to hear and do his will, risking all we have to defeat Satan and to advance the kingdom of God.

APPENDIX A
SIGNS AND WONDERS IN CHURCH HISTORY

Though only a sampling, the following material documents signs and wonders through the centuries. I have limited my sources to major personalities and movements, with few illustrations of lesser-known people. For further reading and documentation, I refer you to the bibliography.

I have separated church history into three ages: patristic, medieval, and reformation-modern. The twentieth century warrants a separate treatment, found in Appendix B.

The patristic era, 100 to 600

Justin Martyr (c. 100–165)

Justin was a Christian apologist who had studied all the great philosophies of his day. In his *Second Apology* (c. 153), Justin, in speaking about the names, meaning, and power of God and Christ, writes concerning exorcism and healing:

> For numberless demoniacs throughout the whole world, and in your city, many of our Christian men exorcising them in the name of Jesus Christ, who was crucified under Pontius Pilate, have healed and do heal, rendering helpless and driving the possessing devils out of the men, though they could not be cured by all the other exorcists, and those who used incantations and drugs. (Coxe 6:190)

In Justin's *Dialogue with Trypho* (a learned Jew), he refers to the current use of spiritual gifts:

For the prophetical gifts remain with us, even to the present time. And hence you ought to understand that [the gifts] formerly among your nation have been transferred to us. (Coxe 1:240)

. . . I have already said, and do again say, that it has been prophesied that this would be done by Him after His ascension to heaven. It is accordingly said, 'He ascended on high, He led captivity captive, He gave gifts unto the sons of men.' And again, in another prophecy it is said 'And it shall come to pass after, I will pour out My Spirit on all flesh, and on My servants, and on My handmaids, and they shall prophesy.' . . . Now, it is possible to see amongst us women and men who possess gifts of the Spirit of God . . . (Coxe 1:243)

Irenaeus (140–203)

Irenaeus was the Bishop of Lyons. His five books *Against Heresies* are devoted to the heresy of Gnosticism. In refuting it he says:

For some do certainly and truly drive out devils, so that those who have thus been cleansed from evil spirits frequently join themselves to the Church. Others have foreknowledge of things to come: they see visions, and utter prophetic expressions. Others still, heal the sick by laying their hands upon them, and they are made whole. Yea, moreover, as I have said, the dead even have been raised up, and remained among us for many years. And what shall I more say? It is not possible to name the number of the gifts which the Church, [scattered] throughout the whole world, has received from God, in the name of Jesus Christ.

Tertullian (c. 160/170–c. 215/220)

Not many details are known concerning Tertullian's life. He was reared in the cultured paganism of Carthage. He became a Christian and joined the Montanist group about 206. He was a prolific writer. In his work *To Scapula*, Chapter 5, he gives this account of expelling demons and healing:

. . . All this might be officially brought under your notice, and by the very advocates, who are themselves also under obligations to us, although in court they give their voice as it suits them. The clerk of one of them who was liable to be thrown upon the ground by an evil spirit, was set free from his affliction; and was also the relative of another, and the little boy of a third. How many men of rank (to say nothing of common people) have been delivered from devils,

and healed of diseases! Even Severus himself, the father of Anto-
nine, was graciously mindful of the Christians; for he sought out
the Christian Proculus, surnamed Torpacion, the steward of Euho-
dias, and in gratitude for his having once cured him by anointing,
he kept him in his palace till the day of his death. (Coxe 3:107)

Novatian (210–280)

Novatian of Rome is noted for two reasons: he was the antipope of the
puritan party in the church, and he gave the Western church its first
full-length treatment of the Trinity. In chapter 29 of *Treatise Concerning the Trinity* he writes of the Spirit:

> This is He who places prophets in the Church, instructs teachers,
> directs tongues, gives powers and healings, does wonderful works,
> offers discrimination of spirits, affords powers of government,
> suggests counsels, and orders and arranges whatever other gifts
> there are of *charismata*; and thus make the Lord's Church every-
> where, and in all, perfected and completed. (Coxe 5:641)

Antony (c. 251–356)

Our knowledge of Antony depends largely on his biography, written by
Athanasius. Chapter forty of this biography shows Antony's work with
the supernatural, especially in dealing with demons:

> Once, a very tall demon appeared with a procession of evil spirits
> and said boldly: 'I am the power of God, I am His providence.
> What do you wish that I grant you?' I then blew my breath at him,
> calling on the name of Christ, and I tried to strike him. I seemed to
> have succeeded, for, immediately, vast as he was, he and all his
> demons disappeared at the name of Christ.

Hilarion (c. 291–371)

Hilarion was an ascetic, educated and converted at Alexandria. By the
time he had been in the desert for twenty-two years, he became widely
known by reputation throughout the cities of Palestine. Jerome, in his
Life of Saint Hilarion, tells of a number of the miracles, healings, and
expulsions of demons that occurred during his ministry:

> Facidia is a small suburb of Rhinocorura, a city of Egypt. From this
> village, a woman who had been blind for ten years was brought to
> be blessed by Hilarion. On being presented to him by the brothers

(already there were many monks with him), she told him that she had bestowed all her substance on physicians. To her the saint replied: 'If what you lost on physicians you had given to the poor, Jesus the true Physician would have healed you'. Whereupon she cried aloud and implored him to have mercy on her. Then, following the example of the Saviour, he rubbed spittle upon her eyes and she was immediately cured. (15: 254–255)

Jerome concludes the section which he devoted to telling of Hilarion's life by stating, 'There would not be time if I wanted to tell you all the signs and wonders performed by Hilarion . . .' (15:262–263)

Macrina the Younger (c. 328–379/380)

Macrina was the sister of Basil, Bishop of Caesarea, and also of Gregory, bishop of Nyssa. Gregory tells of the following healing:

There was with us our little girl who was suffering from an eye ailment resulting from an infectious sickness. It was a terrible and pitiful thing to see her as the membrane around the pupil was swollen and whitened by the disease.

I went to the men's quarters where your brother Peter was Superior, and my wife went to the women's quarters to be with St. Macrina. After an interval of time we were getting ready to leave but the blessed one would not let my wife go, and said she would not give up my daughter, whom she was holding in her arms, until she had given them a meal and offered them 'the wealth of philosophy'. She kissed the child as one might expect and put her lips on her eyes and, when she noticed the diseased pupil she said, 'If you do me the favour of remaining for dinner I will give you a return in keeping with this honour'. When the child's mother asked what it was, the great lady replied, 'I have some medicine which is especially effective in curing eye disease.'

We gladly remained and later started the journey home, bright and happy. Each of us told his own story on the way. My wife was telling everything in order, as if going through a treatise, and when she came to the point at which the medicine was promised, interrupting the narrative, she said, 'What have we done? How did we forget the promise, the medicine for the eyes?'

I was annoyed at our thoughtlessness, and quickly sent one of my men back to ask for the medicine, when the child, who happened to be in her nurse's arms, looked at her mother, and the mother, fixing her gaze on the child's eyes said, 'Stop being upset by our carelessness.' She said this in a loud voice, joyfully and fearfully.

'Nothing of what was promised to us has been omitted, but the true medicine that heals diseases, the cure that comes from prayer, this she has given us, and has already worked; nothing at all is left of the disease of the eyes.'

As she said this, she took our child and put her in my arms, and I also then comprehended the miracles in the gospel which I had not believed before, and I said, 'What a great thing it is for sight to be restored to the blind by the hand of God, if now his handmaiden makes such cures and has done such a thing through faith in him, a fact no less impressive than these miracles'.

Ambrose (c. 339–397)

Ambrose was the bishop of Milan. When ordained as a bishop his first act was to distribute his wealth among the poor. He was an outstanding preacher and teacher, and very outspoken.

Ambrose, in *The Holy Spirit (Fathers of the Church)* states that healings and tongues were still given by God:

. . . Behold, the Father established the teachers; Christ also established them in the churches; and just as the Father gives the grace of healings, so the Son also gives it; just as the Father gives the gift of tongues, so the Son also has bestowed it. (Deferrari 44:150)

Augustine (354–430)

Augustine was bishop of Hippo and the greatest of the Latin Fathers. He was baptised by Ambrose in Milan on Easter 387.

At the close of his life, he wrote *The City of God* (c. 413–427). In Book 22, chapter 28, Augustine details the miracles which were occurring in his day: 'It is sometimes objected that the miracles, which Christians claimed to have occurred, no longer happen'. He argues that the ones which happened and were recorded in the New Testament are 'absolutely trustworthy'. Then he writes, 'The truth is that even today miracles are being wrought in the name of Christ, sometimes through His sacraments and sometimes through the intercession of the relics of His saints'.

Augustine then tells of the miracles which have happened. (Deferrari 24:431–445).

– A blind man whose sight was restored (24:433).
– The Bishop Innocent in Carthage healed of a rectal fistula (24:433–437).
– Innocentia in Carthage healed of breast cancer (24:437–438).
– A doctor in Carthage healed of gout (24:438–439).

- An ex-showman of Curcubis healed of paralysis and a hernia in the scrotum (24:439).
- The healing of Hesperius, one of Augustine's neighbours, whose diseases were caused by 'evil spirits' (24:439).
- A demonised boy cured, after the demon ripped out his eye and left it 'hanging by a tiny vein as by a root. The pupil which was black, turned white' (24:440–441).
- A young girl in Hippo delivered from demons (24:441).
- Florentius of Hippo who prayed for money and received it (24:441–442).
- A blind woman healed in Hippo (24:442).
- Bishop Lucillus of Synity healed of a fistula (24:442–443).
- Eucharius, a Spanish priest, possibly brought back from the dead (24:443).
- Martila – healed and saved (24:443–444).
- Three healed of gout (24:444).
- A child, who was run over by a cart, healed with no sign of being run over (24:444).
- The resuscitation of a nun (24:444).
- The resuscitation of a Syrian's daughter (24:444).
- Augustine's friend's son who was raised from the dead (24:445).

Augustine ends his narrative of miracles by telling his readers that there are too many miracles to list.

'It is a simple fact', Augustine writes, 'that there is no lack of miracles even in our day. And the God who works the miracles we read of in the scriptures uses any means and manner he chooses'.

Gregory of Tours (c. 538–594)

Gregory was a bishop and historian. He was a prolific writer, whose works provide invaluable knowledge of sixth century church life (Douglas 1974, 436). There are many accounts of healings which occurred in Gregory's time. They are to be found in his *Dialogues* where he relates the expelling of a demon and his own healing:

Eleutherius, whom I mentioned previously, abbot of the Monastery of St. Mark, the Evangelist adjoining the walls of Spoleto, lived with me for a long time in my monastery at Rome and died there. His disciples say that he raised a dead person to life by the power of his prayer. He was well known for his simplicity and compunction of heart, and undoubtedly through his tears this humble, childlike soul obtained many favours from almighty God.

I will tell you about a miracle of his which I had him describe to me in his own simple words. Once while he was travelling, evening came on before he could find a lodging for the night, so he stopped at a convent. There was a little boy in this convent who was troubled every night by an evil spirit. So, after welcoming the man of God to their convent, the nuns asked him to keep the boy with him that night. He agreed, and allowed the boy to rest near him. In the morning the nuns asked him with deep concern whether he had done anything for the boy. Rather surprised that they should ask, he said, 'No'. Then they acquainted him with the boy's condition, informing him that not a night passed without the evil spirit troubling the boy. Would Eleutherius please take him along to the monastery because they could no longer bear to see him suffer. The man of God agreed to do so.

The boy remained a long time in the monastery without being troubled in the least. Highly pleased at this, the old abbot allowed his joy at the boy's healthy condition to exceed moderation. 'Brothers', he said to his monks, 'the Devil had his joke with the sisters, but once he encountered real servants of God, he no longer dared to come near this boy'. That very instant, hardly waiting for Eleutherius to finish speaking, the Devil again took possession of the young boy, tormenting him in the presence of all. The sight of it filled the old man's heart with grief, and when his monks tried to console him he said, 'Upon my word! Not one of you shall taste bread today until this boy is snatched out of the Devil's power'.

He prostrated himself in prayer with all his monks and continued praying until the boy was freed from the power of the evil spirit. The cure was complete and the Devil did not dare molest him any further.

Gregory I (the Great) (540–604)

Gregory the Great was the pope from 590 to 604. His *Dialogues* (593–94) were described by the author himself as stories of 'the miracles of the Fathers which were done in Italy'. The *Dialogues* contain supernatural tales, dividing neatly into three classes: stories of visions, stories of prophecies, and stories of miracles.

The following, a summary of one of Gregory's stories, is taken from Frederick Dudden's seminal work on the life of Gregory:

One day at Subiaco, the little monk Placidus, the future Apostle of his [Gregory's] Order in Sicily, went to the lake to draw water, but overbalanced himself and fell in. Benedict, who was sitting in his cell, was supernaturally aware of the occurrence, and cried out hastily to his disciple Maurus: 'Run, Brother Maurus, for the child who went to fetch water has fallen into the lake, and the stream has

carried him a great way.' Maurus ran down to the edge of the lake,
and then, 'thinking still that he went on dry land, he ran on the
water', caught the drifting boy by the hair and brought him safely
back. It was only when he stood again on the firm ground that
Maurus realised that a miracle had taken place, and 'much astonished, he wondered how he had done that which knowingly he
would not have dared to venture.' (Dudden, vol. I 1905, 334)

The medieval era, 600 to 1500

St. Francis of Assisi (1181–1226)

St. Francis was the founder of the Franciscan Order. He had an
extensive healing ministry. The following selections are taken from a
vast number of miracles that occurred in the ministry of Francis:

> Once when the holy man of God Francis was going about through
> various regions to preach the kingdom of God, he came to a certain
> city called Toscanella. There, when he was sowing the seed of life
> in his usual way, a certain soldier of that city gave him hospitality;
> he had an only son who was lame and weak of body. Though he was
> a young child, he had passed the years of weaning; still he remained
> in a cradle. When the father of the boy saw the great sanctity of the
> man of God, he humbly cast himself at his feet, begging from him
> health for his son. But Francis, who considered himself useless and
> unworthy of such great power and grace, refused for a long time to
> do this. But finally overcome by the insistence of his petitions, he
> prayed and then put his hand upon the boy and, blessing him,
> raised him up. Immediately, with all present looking on and
> rejoicing, the boy arose completely restored and began to walk
> here and there about the house.
>
> Once when the man of God Francis had come to Narni and was
> staying there for a number of days, a certain man of that city, Peter
> by name, lay in bed paralysed. For a period of five months he had
> been so deprived of the use of all his limbs that he could not rise at
> all or move himself even a little; and thus having completely lost
> the use of his feet and hands and head, he could only move his
> tongue and open his eyes. When he heard that Francis had come to
> Narni, he sent a messenger to the bishop of that city to ask him for
> the love of God to send the servant of the most high God to him,
> confident that he would be freed from the illness from which he
> suffered at the sight and presence of Francis. And so it happened
> that, when the blessed Francis had come to him and had made the
> sign of the cross over him from his head to his feet, he was

immediately healed and restored to his former health. (Hermann nd., 59–60)

Waldensian Community

This was a movement in the Middle Ages whose characteristics included evangelical obedience to the gospel, rigorous asceticism, aversion to recognising the ministry of unworthy-living priests, belief in visions, prophecies, and spirit possession (Douglas 1974, 1026). A. J. Gordon, in his book *The Ministry of Healing*, quotes the following doctrine of the Waldensians:

> Therefore, concerning this anointing of the sick, we hold it *as an article of faith*, and profess sincerely from the heart that sick persons, when they ask it, may lawfully be anointed with the anointing oil by one who joins them in praying that it may be efficacious to the healing of the body according to the design and end and effect mentioned by the apostles; and we profess that such an anointing performed according to the apostolic design and practice will be healing and profitable. (Gordon 1802, 65)

Vincent Ferrer (1350–1419)

Vincent was a Dominican preacher who was born in Valencia. Known as the 'Angel of the Judgement', he preached across Europe for almost twenty years. The *New Catholic Encyclopedia* records the following:

> Vincent was disillusioned; he became gravely ill. In a vision, he was commissioned by the Lord, who was accompanied by St. Dominic and St. Francis, 'to go through the world preaching Christ.' After a year had passed Benedict permitted him to go. In November 1399, therefore, he set forth from Avignon and spent 20 years in apostolic preaching. As the spirit moved him or as he was requested, he visited and revisited places throughout Spain, southern France, Lombardy, Switzerland, northern France, and the low countries. With fiery eloquence he preached the need of repentance and the coming of the Judgement. He seldom remained in any one place for more than a day, and then only when the people had been long neglected or when heresy or paganism was rife. Miracles in the order of nature and of grace accompanied his steps. (14:681)

The *Catholic Encyclopedia Dictionary* also notes: 'He is said by some to have had the gift of tongues . . .' (1002)

Colette of Corbi (d. 1447)

The following is recorded about Colette in *The Lives of the Saints*:

> In 1410, she founded a convent at Besancon; in 1415, she intro-
> duced a reform into the convent of the Cordeliers, at Dole, and in
> succession into nearly all the convents in Lorraine, Champagne,
> and Picardy. In 1416, she founded a house of her order at Poligny,
> at the foot of the Jura, and another at Auxonne. 'I am dying of
> curiosity to see this wonderful Colette, who resuscitates the dead',
> wrote the Duchess of Bourbon, about this time. For the fame of the
> miracles and labours of the carpenter's daughter was in every
> mouth. (Baring-Gould 1897, 3:99–100)

Reformation and modern era, 1500 to 1900

Martin Luther (1483–1546)

In *Luther: Letters of Spiritual Counsel*, the following letter of Martin
Luther is recorded:

> The tax collector in Torgau and the counsellor in Belgern have
> written me to ask that I offer some good advice and help for Mrs.
> John Korner's afflicted husband. I know of no worldly help to give.
> If the physicians are at a loss to find a remedy, you may be sure that
> it is not a case of ordinary melancholy. It must, rather, be an
> affliction that comes from the devil, and this must be counteracted
> by the power of Christ with the prayer of faith. This is what we do,
> and what we have been accustomed to do, for a cabinet maker here
> was similarly afflicted with madness and we cured him by prayer in
> Christ's name.
>
> Accordingly you should proceed as follows: Go to him with the
> deacon and two or three good men. Confident that you, as pastor of
> the place, are clothed with the authority of the ministerial office,
> lay your hands upon him and say, 'Peace be with you, dear brother,
> from God our Father and from our Lord Jesus Christ'. Thereupon
> repeat the Creed and the Lord's Prayer over him in a clear voice,
> and close with these words: 'O God, almighty Father, who hast told
> us through thy Son, "Verily, verily I say unto you, Whatsoever ye
> shall ask the Father in my name, he will give it you"; who hast
> commanded and encouraged us to pray in his name, "Ask, and ye
> shall receive", and who in like manner hast said, "Call upon me in
> the day of trouble: I will deliver thee, and thou shalt glorify me";
> we unworthy sinners, relying on these thy words and commands,
> pray for thy mercy with such faith as we can muster. Graciously

deign to free this man from all evil, and put to nought the work that Satan has done in him, to the honour of thy name and the strengthening of the faith of believers; through the same Jesus Christ, thy Son, our Lord, who liveth and reigneth with thee, world without end. Amen'. Then, when you depart, lay your hands upon the man again and say, 'These signs shall follow them that believe; they shall lay hands on the sick, and they shall recover'. Do this three times, once on each of three successive days. (Tappert nd. 18:52)

In *Luther's Works*, concerning prophecy, he says, 'If you wish to prophesy, do it in such a way that it does not go beyond faith so that your prophesying can be in harmony with the peculiar quality of faith'. He goes on to write that 'one may prophesy new things but not things that go beyond the bounds of faith . . .' (Oswald nd. 25:444–451)

Ignatius of Loyola (1491–1556)

Ignatius was the founder of the Society of Jesus. He was wounded in the Spanish army in 1521. While recuperating he read the *Life of Christ* by Ludolph of Saxony. This inspired him to become a 'soldier' for Christ. He entered a monastery and spent nearly a year at ascetic practices. Here he composed the essence of *Spiritual Exercises*. In them he writes the following about the Spirit:

The Spirit of God breathes where he will; he does not ask our permission; he meets us on his own terms and distributes his charisms as He pleases. Therefore, we must always be awake and ready; we must be pliable so that he can use us in new enterprises. We cannot lay down the law to the Spirit of God! He is only present with his gifts where he knows that they are joined with the multiplicity of charisms in the one Church. All the gifts of this church stem from one source – God. What Paul says in the twelfth chapter of his First Epistle to the Corinthians is still true today! This should give us the strength to overcome every form of clerical jealousy, mutual suspicion, power-grabbing, and the refusal to let others – who have their own gifts of the Spirit – go on their own way. That is what the Spirit wants from us! He is not so narrow-minded as we sometimes are with our recipes! He can lead to himself in different ways, and He wants to direct the church through a multiplicity of functions, offices, and gifts. The church is not supposed to be a military academy in which everything is uniform, but she is supposed to be the body of Christ in which he, the one Spirit, exerts his power in all the members. Each one of these members proves that he really is a member of this body by letting the other members be. (Rahner 1962, 254–255)

Teresa of Avila (1515–1582)

Teresa was born in Spain and educated by Augustinian nuns. She was a Carmelite reformer, mystic, and writer. In her autobiography there are frequent accounts of the ecstasy she had experienced from God. In chapter twelve, verse five, she writes, 'What I say about not ascending to God unless he raises one up is language of the Spirit. He who has had some experience will understand me, for I don't know how to describe this being raised up if it isn't understood through experience'. In chapter 16:1–2, she refers to this kind of speech again when talking about prayer:

> I don't know any other terms for describing it or how to explain it. Nor does the soul then know what to do because it doesn't know whether to speak or to be silent, whether to laugh or to weep. This prayer is a glorious foolishness, a heavenly madness where the true wisdom is learned; and it is for the soul a most delightful way of enjoying. In fact five or even six years ago the Lord often gave me this prayer in abundance, and I didn't understand it; nor did I know how to speak of it. (109)

Valentine Greatlakes (d. 1638)

David Robertson writes in his article 'From Epidauros to Lourdes: A History of Healing by Faith' about an Irishman named Greatlakes:

> He was a Protestant in Catholic Ireland and fled to England in 1641 at the outbreak of the Irish Rebellion. For a time he served under Cromwell. In 1661, after a period of depression, he came to believe that God had given him, a mere commoner, the power to cure scrofula. When he began trying to cure the king's evil, his friends and acquaintances were astounded to find that he did indeed seem able to produce a regression in this disease. This stunning achievement led him to try his hand at other illnesses like epilepsy, paralysis, deafness, ulcers, and diverse nervous disorders, and he found that his touch was efficacious in these cases as well. Soon word of his uncanny ability spread far and wide and he was besieged by multitudes of sick people. The crowds that came to him were so great that he could not accommodate all of them even if he worked from six in the morning until six at night. (Frazier 1973, 187)

The Quakers, or The Society of Friends (1640–present)

The Quakers' origins are traced back to English Puritanism in the 1640s. The first leader was George Fox who preached a message of the New Age of the Spirit. They were opposed by both the Puritans and Anglicans. The typical Quaker meeting was characterised by the people waiting for the Spirit to speak through them, and by the people 'quaking' as God moved among them. The following are some excerpts from Fox's *Journal*:

> In the year 1648, as I was sitting in a friend's house in Nottingham-shire (for by this time the power of God had opened the hearts of some to receive the word of life and reconciliation), I saw there was a great crack to go throughout the earth, and a great smoke to go as the crack went; and that after the crack there should be a great shaking: this was the earth in people's hearts, which was to be shaken before the seed of God was raised out of the earth. And it was so: for the Lord's power began to shake them, and great meetings we begun to have, and mighty power and work of God there was amongst people, to the astonishment of both people and priests. (Fox 1901, 23)

The Huguenots (Formally organised in 1559)

Huguenots was a nickname for the French Calvinists. Henry Baird writes the following concerning some of the phenomena of this religious group.

> Respecting the physical manifestations, there is little discrepancy between the accounts of friend and foe. The persons affected were men and women, the old and the young. Very many were children, boys and girls of nine or ten years of age. They were sprung from the people – their enemies said, from the dregs of the people – ignorant and uncultured; for the most part unable to read or write, and speaking in everyday life the *patois* of the province with which alone they were conversant. Such persons would suddenly fall backward, and, while extended at full length on the ground, undergo strange and apparently involuntary contortions; their chests would seem to heave, their stomachs to inflate. On coming gradually out of this condition, they appeared instantly to regain the power of speech. Beginning often in a voice interrupted by sobs, they soon poured forth a torrent of words – cries for mercy, calls to repentance, exhortations to the bystanders to cease frequenting the mass, denunciations of the church of Rome, proph-

ecies of coming judgement. From the mouths of those that were little more than babes came texts of Scripture, and discourse in good and intelligible French, such as they never used in their conscious hours. When the trance ceased, they declared that they remembered nothing of what had occurred, or of what they had said. In rare cases they retained a general and vague impression, but nothing more. There was no appearance of deceit or collusion, and no indication that in uttering their predictions respecting coming events they had any thought of prudence, or doubt as to the truth of what they foretold. Brueys, their most inveterate opponent, is not less positive on this point than are the witnesses who are most favourable to them. 'These poor madmen', he said, 'believed that they were indeed inspired by the Holy Ghost. They prophesied without any (ulterior) design, without evil intent, and with so little reserve, that they always boldly marked the day, the place and persons of whom they spoke in their predictions'. (2:186–187)

Jansenists (c. 1731)

'The expectation of miracles and other supernatural signs had become almost an integral part of the Jansenist worldview by the end of the seventeenth century', wrote Robert Kreiser in his book *Miracles, Convulsions, and Ecclesiastical Politics in Early Eighteenth Century Paris*.

One such miracle that he records is the cure of Pascal's niece in March 1656. Marguerite had been suffering for a long time from a serious and disfiguring lachrymal fistula in the corner of her eye. She was healed when a Holy Thorn was simply touched to her eye. The miracle was supported by substantial medical evidence and made a profound impression on the public.

John Wesley (1703–1791)

John Wesley was the founder of the Methodist Church. In his *Journal* he writes:

Wed., Aug. 15, 1750 – By reflecting on an odd book which I had read in this journey, *The General Delusion of Christians with Regard to Prophecy*, I was fully convinced of what I had once suspected: (1) That the Montanists, in the second and third centuries, were real, scriptural Christians; and (2) That the grand reason why the miraculous gifts were so soon withdrawn, was not only that faith and holiness were wellnigh lost, but that dry, formal, orthodox men began even then to ridicule whatever gifts they had not themselves, and to decry them all as either madness or imposture.

Wesley wrote a letter to Thomas Church in June 1746 in which he states:

Yet I do not know that God hath anyway precluded himself from thus exerting His sovereign power from working miracles in any kind or degree in any age to the end of the world. I do not recollect any scripture wherein we are taught that miracles were to be confined within the limits either of the apostolic or the Cyprianic age, or of any period of time, longer or shorter, even till the restitution of all things. I have not observed, either in the Old Testament, or the New, any intimation at all of this kind. St. Paul says, indeed, once, concerning two of the miraculous gifts of the Spirit (so, I think, that test is usually understood), 'Whether there be prophecies, they shall fail; whether there be tongues, they shall cease.' But he does not say, either that these or any other miracles shall cease till faith and hope shall cease also, till they all be swallowed up in the vision of God, and love be all in all. (Telford nd. 2:261)

Lourdes (1858–present)

Lourdes, in France, had religious events which gave birth to the phenomena which have occurred there. These 'religious events' began between February 11 and July 16, 1858. A control group was established in 1882 to handle all the material regarding the cases of miraculous cures. Between 1918 and 1956, 216 cases of miracles were recorded. A complete overview of this subject may be found in Monden's *Signs and Wonders*, pp. 194–250, where several detailed studies of the miracles are given. The cases include cures of cancer, tuberculosis, blindness, and various other diseases.

Azusa Street (1906)

In 1905, Charles Parham moved his school to Houston, Texas. There William J. Seymour, a black evangelist, joined the school. He embraced the 'teaching on tongues' but did not experience this in Houston. In 1906, Seymour was invited to speak in a small black Nazarene church in Los Angeles. On April 1, 1906, Seymour spoke in tongues. The small group soon outgrew the little house on Bonnie Brae and moved into an old livery stable at 312 Azusa Street.

Seymour was the central figure of the Azusa Street Revival. The

Revival continued for three and a half years at Azusa Street. Services were held three times daily – morning, afternoon, and evening. Tongues speaking was a central attraction, but healing of the sick was not far behind. Seymour became the pastor of the congregation, which was made up of both blacks and whites, until his death in 1929. Pilgrims to Azusa were common and came from all parts of the world. (*Azusa Street*, pp. 136).

APPENDIX B
SIGNS AND WONDERS IN THE
TWENTIETH CENTURY

Signs and wonders are still occurring in this century, both in and out of the immediate supervision of Western denominations. Indications are that churches grow most rapidly where Western Christians – and their antisupernatural bent – have the least immediate influence.

The following are random case studies gathered by myself and others. I only recount examples that demonstrate the relationship between signs and wonders and church growth.

South Africa

In South Africa there is an Indian community of about 800,000 that was solidly opposed to the Christian faith. Very few Indians became Christians. About twenty or twenty-five years ago, through a series of healing campaigns, two Pentecostal denominations began to grow among the Indians. One of those Pentecostal churches is now 25,000 strong, the other 15,000.[1]

Reinhard Bonnke

Bonnke is a German missionary ministering through an independent organisation called Christ For All Nations, mainly in the black homelands of South Africa.

His first campaign was conducted in Gaberones, Botswana, with the Apostolic Faith Mission (A.F.M.) that at that time had only forty members in the city. Nightly after preaching, Bonnke would be joined by Richard Ngidi to pray for the sick. After only six days they were attracting crowds of 2,000 to an auditorium that seated 800. Dramatic healings resulted and the meetings were moved to a stadium where they attracted a nightly audience of 10,000 people.

The next campaign was held in Sibasa, northern Transvaal. Within seven days after the occurrence of extraordinary miracles, the stadium was filled with a nightly audience of 30,000 people, despite heavy rains.

In 1979, Bonnke held a campaign for the A.F.M. in Bloemfontein, South Africa. Hundreds were saved, healed, and baptised in water. After a campaign of twenty days they planted a new church with a baptised membership of over 600 people. Christ For All Nations have now built a tent that accommodates 34,000 people, and are using it regularly.[2]

Erlo Stegen

Stegen is a German missionary working with the Zulus in Kwasizabantu in South Africa. The first twelve years of his ministry in their region were completely unsuccessful. At that point, totally frustrated, Stegen began a detailed study of the book of Acts with a group of black associates. They identified signs and wonders as being the key to the rapid growth of the early church. Later they experienced the filling of the Holy Spirit. The details of that experience were described as being similar to the account in Acts 2.

Immediately after leaving the room where they had experienced the anointing of the Holy Spirit, Stegen and the group were met by a demon-possessed woman who said, 'Something just drove me to come here and ask you to pray for me.' They cast the demon out, the woman being delivered and set free. The woman returned to her village and caused a small revival. She preached the gospel, prayed for the sick, and hundreds that had known her before gave their lives to the Lord.

From that point on people began streaming to Kwasizabantu. Every time a person was healed, saved, and filled with the Spirit, he or she went back to their own village and proclaimed the gospel there. This was the start of a large revival.[3]

Ivory Coast

Prophet Harris

The prophet William Wade Harris, a Liberian of the Berbos tribe, grew up under the influence of Christianity. His uncle was a Methodist preacher in Liberia. At the age of twenty, Harris had a deep religious experience. However, his Christian ministry did not begin until he was sixty years old.

In 1913, 'Prophet Harris' as he was called, entered the Ivory Coast to embark on one of the greatest evangelistic tours ever recorded in African history. Rene Bureau, in his unpublished dissertation, 'The Prophet Harris', adds some insight on the way God called Prophet Harris to become a missionary. He reveals the testimony given to a Catholic priest in the Ivory Coast before Harris started his journey along the coast:

I am a prophet of God. Four years ago I was awakened at night. I saw my guardian angel under my bed. He hit me three times on the forehead, saying, 'I am going to take your wife from you. She will die, but I will give you many people to help you. Before your wife dies, she will give you six shillings, that will be your fortune. You will never need anything. I will be with you always and reveal to you the mission of God.' That's why I have come. I am here to do God's mission.

William Harris then began his journey along the coastline of the Ivory Coast. He dressed in a white robe and turban, carried a Bible, a bamboo cross, and a gourd of water. He went everywhere proclaiming the message of salvation in Christ. He never read from the Bible, because the people were illiterate. He quoted from memory passages dealing with salvation. He taught songs and proclaimed that the worship of fetishes and idols was wrong and that God would punish people who practised such things. He challenged the people to burn their fetishes and follow God.

Harris would invite those wanting to follow God to come forward and kneel before the cross. They would come and place both hands on the bamboo cross, confessing their sins. Harris would then touch the tops of their heads with his Bible. The new converts would tremble, and Harris would expel demons.

In Jackville, Harris healed the chief's wife who was dying. He said, 'Touch this cross, get up, and walk'. She did, and the entire village was converted.

He organised groups of believers and advised them to construct chapels. He placed a pastor in charge of each and had each group select twelve apostles to direct the church. Some converts were sent to the interior tribes to bring them the message of salvation. Harris told these newly-formed congregations that missionaries would come to explain the Bible.

After two years of ministry in the Ivory Coast, Harris was arrested by the French authorities and sent back to Liberia. The French feared this new religious movement and attempted to stop it.[4]

Jacques Giraud

The Church in Ivory Coast was typical of many countries of Asia, Africa, and Latin America. The Ivory Coast has about four million people, with the Roman Catholic Church claiming about 30,000. The Methodist Church dates from 1924 and has 60,000. Seven small Protestant denominations, with a total baptised membership of about 11,000, have arisen because of the faithful work of missionaries. Their growth rate is seventy percent per decade. (About 150 dedicated missionaries from America, Switzerland, and France are helping these churches and are doing a multitude of good deeds.)

Pastor Jacques Giraud, a French missionary to the West Indies, arrived in the Ivory Coast in March 1973 to dedicate an Assemblies of God church building in Abidjan. As the meetings progressed, people began to be healed. The crowds grew and the meetings were moved to the stadium. Truck loads of people came from all parts of the Ivory Coast. The papers and radio stations reported the events. Leading government officials and their wives flocked to the stadium.

Pastor Giraud would tell about one of Christ's miracles and preach for an hour on God's mighty power to heal. Then he would say, 'I don't heal. God heals. I ask him to release his power. Put your hand where it hurts and join me in prayer'. He would pour out his heart in believing prayer to God for healing. After a half hour of prayer he would invite those whom God had healed to come to the front. Crutches were thrown away. Bent and arthritic persons stood erect. Blind men walked forward seeing. Scores and sometimes hundreds came. God had given them at least a measure of healing. (Thousands were also not healed.)

Although he was a minister of the Assemblies of God denomination, it was his practice to direct converts to the local churches and missions for shepherding. At Toumoudi he had the Christian and Missionary Alliance missionaries and ministers on the platform with him. He said to the people, 'When you place your faith in Jesus Christ, call these men to baptise you and shepherd you'.

Reverend Fred Pilding, a missionary of the Christian and Missionary Alliance working in the Ivory Coast fills in some details in the *Alliance Witness*, September 26, 1973:

> The crusade began in Bouake on June 18th and continued for three weeks. Morning attendance averaged about 4,000. From 6,000 to 15,000 turned out in the evenings with a high of 25,000 one Sunday. The sick were seated on the grass on the playing field, and all the others occupied the grandstands. As the evangelist presented Jesus Christ, the same yesterday, today, and forever, people became aware of his continuing power today, through a healing receptive place. It became easier for them to trust him as Saviour.

A hunchback came to the meeting, grovelling in the dirt, under the influence of demons. The demons were exorcised in the name of Jesus and he was instantly healed. The next day he attended the meetings nicely dressed, perfectly calm, and gave his testimony.

Whenever those who were healed testified, witnesses were asked to verify each healing. Pastor Giraud again and again cited Mark 16:15–18 as every believer's commission and emphasised that in Christ's name they were to cast out devils and lay hands on the sick and they shall recover. He refuted vigorously the title of healer. His ministry, he said, was to inspire faith in the gospel. 'It is in the name of Jesus that people are healed.'

After the Toumoudi meeting, groups of converts from 81 villages around Toumoudi sought out the Alliance missionaries and ministers, begging them to come and make them Christians. After the Bouake meeting, responses were received from over 100 villages. A hundred and forty cards were filled out from one small town alone.

From one village near Bouake ten cards had been received. The missionary went to visit this village. Seeing him, one of the men who had been healed rushed off to get some of the pagan village elders. While waiting, the missionary said to the children, 'Do you know Pastor Giraud's song?' Immediately they broke into joyful singing, 'Up, up with Jesus, down, down with Satan, Alleluia!' People came pouring out and the missionary preached and then asked, 'How many will follow God and leave their old ways?' More than half immediately said, 'We will'. In another village the Chief said, 'Fetish is dead, we shall all become Christians'.

The pastors and missionaries were faced with great opportunities. The challenge was to take advantage of this enthusiasm, which could dissipate rapidly, and channel these people into ongoing responsible churches of Christians who know the Lord, obey his word. Nothing like this had happened in their experience on the Ivory Coast, and they were naturally fearful, lest the excitement prove transient as it very well might.[5]

Argentina

Tommy Hicks

In 1952, God spoke to American evangelist Tommy Hicks through a vision, telling him to go to South America and preach the gospel. In 1954, while on his way to Buenos Aires, the name Peron flashed into Hicks' mind. He knew nobody by that name. Near the flight's destination he asked the stewardess whether she knew anybody by that name. She replied, 'Yes, Mr. Peron is the President of Argentina.' Hicks sought an appointment with Mr. Peron but ran into difficulties. Then an extraordinary event took place at the President's office. While seeking an interview, Hicks encountered Mr. Peron's secretary, who had a bad leg. Hicks prayed for him and he was instantly healed. This resulted in Hicks being introduced to General Peron.

Peron received Hicks warmly and instructed his assistant to give Hicks whatever he asked for. On Hicks' request, a large stadium was made available to him as well as free access to the government controlled radio and press. The campaign lasted for fifty-two days. Hicks preached the gospel on the saving power of Jesus, emphasising divine healing. Over two million people attended the meetings. Some 200,000 people attended the campaign on the final night. Although almost all the local churches grew as a result of the campaign, the Assemblies of God gained the most. Their growth, from 174 in 1951 to nearly 2,000 members in 1956, reflects the tremendous impact of Hicks' campaign.[6]

India

Suba Rao was the headmaster of a government school in India, a member of one of the middle castes and a wealthy man. He hated missionaries and laughed at baptism. He thought of the church as an assembly of the low caste (which, from a socio-economic standpoint, it was).

One of his near neighbours and close friends fell sick. For two years his sickness was not healed. The friend was gradually wasting away. He went to many doctors, to no avail. One night, while Suba Rao was asleep, the Lord Jesus appeared to him and said, 'If you will go and lay your hand on that man's head and pray in my name, I will heal him'. Suba Rao woke up and laughed, thinking, 'What a funny dream', and went back to sleep.

The next night the Lord Jesus stood by his side and said, 'If you go and lay your hand on that man's head and pray for him to be healed, I will heal him'. Suba Rao woke up. He didn't laugh this time, and he didn't go back to sleep; but he didn't lay his hands on the sick man either. He thought, 'That's impossible'. The third night the Lord Jesus appeared to him again. This time he got up at once and went to his neighbour. He laid his hand on the man's head, prayed for him, and in the morning the man said, 'I feel much better. Do it again'. The man was healed.

Suba Rao threw out his idols. He started to read the Bible. He started a Bible study class among his neighbours. Still today he ridicules baptism. He has still not joined any church. But he proclaims himself a follower of the Lord Jesus. The healing of people in Jesus' name has become his chief occupation. Joining the church, which in India is composed largely of the lowest castes of Indian society is, he thinks, an impossible step for him. Still, the Lord Jesus heals men through Suba Rao.[7]

The Nishi Tribals

The Nishi Tribals in Sulansini Division in Northeast India are now receptive to the miraculous. It all started when a high government official's youngest son fell terminally ill:

> A Hindu pharmacist, recognising that the child was beyond medical help, advised that the father 'Try the Christian God, Jesus Christ. I have once heard that he had raised a man called Lazarus, who had already been dead for three days!' As the father approached his house, he heard crying and wailing, and he knew that his son must have died. He went into the house, discovered that it was so, but then went into the son's room, placed his hand on the chest of his dead son and prayed, 'Jesus, I do not know who you are, but I have just heard that you raised Lazarus from the dead after three days. My son has died only a few hours ago, and if you raise him up, I promise you, even though I do not know who you are, my family and I will worship you.' Immediately the eyes of the child began to flicker again and he was restored to life. The impact of the miracle was tremendous. The people cried, 'Jesus, who are you? What love you have for us!' Within the next couple of weeks, hundreds gave their lives to Jesus.[8]

China

David Wang is the General Director of Asian Outreach. He visits mainland China quite often and has regular contact with the believers there. His reports of what the Lord is doing in China are very exciting.

For example, he tells us that near Foochon, there is a place called Christian Mountain. The community of Christian Mountain consists of between 30 and 50,000 people, of whom ninety percent are Christians. The growth of this Christian community can be related directly to the deliverance of a girl possessed by demons during 1969–1970.

Indonesia

The well-known German theologian, Kurt Koch, did some excellent research on what is now called the 'revival in Indonesia'.

Timor is one of the islands at the eastern extremity of Indonesia. Out of a population of one million, some 450,000 people belong to the former Dutch Reformed Church. According to Koch, by the early sixties the spiritual state of the churches was almost catastrophic. Timor had never been evangelised; only 'Christianised'. In 1964, God instructed a man, named Jephtah (a teacher on the island of Rote), in a vision, to travel to Timor and hold a healing campaign there. From the start of the campaign God confirmed Jephtah's calling with a mighty ministry of signs and wonders. Following the close of the campaign, a further week of healing was held in Sol. According to the various reports which were later confirmed, several thousand people were healed. All of this was the start of what developed into a mighty revival, with thousands being saved. In one area an evangelistic team won more than 9,000 people for Christ in just two weeks.

Canada

Red Sucker Lake, Manitoba, 1951

A young couple, new missionaries, were spending their first winter of marriage in this isolated Cree Indian village. It was towards springtime, and lakes and river were clogged with ice, making float flying (landing aeroplanes on lakes) impossible. There was neither telephone nor radio communication to the outside.

The missionaries were in the initial stages of language learning. The small child of a prominent native became very seriously ill. There were no medical facilities in the village. The workers had no medical training. As the child worsened, friends suggested that perhaps the new missionary would pray for the child. The father refused, saying, 'He's a false teacher, how could he do any good?' The days passed and the child's condition became critical until it was clear to all he was dying. The neighbours said, 'Well, it can't hurt now to let him pray for him. The child's dying anyway'. The father reluctantly yielded. The missionary came to the tent, prayed briefly for the child to get well, then left. The next day the child had completely recovered. Today, the grown child is living a normal life, happily married. Eventually, the father was converted, went to Bible school, and became the pastor of the Indian church in the village.[9]

NOTES

Chapter 1

1 Much of this chapter is based on material gleaned from the writings of George Ladd and James Kallas. For those readers interested in further reading on the kingdom of God, I recommend Ladd's *A Theology of the New Testament* (Grand Rapids, Michigan: Eerdmans Publishing Company, 1974) and Kallas's *The Real Satan* (Minneapolis: Augsburg Publishing House, 1975).

2 See Amos 9:14; Isaiah 11; Zechariah 8:4–8.

3 James Kallas, *Jesus and the Power of Satan* (Philadelphia: The Westminster Press, 1968), pages 119–21.

4 It is not my intention to equate the fifteen books of the Apocrypha with canon. In article six of the Thirty-Nine Articles, we read:

> And the other Books (as Hierome [Jerome] saith) the Church doth read for example of life and instruction of manners; but yet doth it not apply them to establish any doctrine.

5 The Hebrew understanding of time was different from that of the Greeks. Rather than thinking of 'eternity' as outside time, or without a beginning or ending (cyclical in nature), the New Testament Greek words that we translate as eternity (*eis ton aiona* – usually translated 'forever') literally mean 'for ages' (also see Mark 3:29; Luke 1:33,55; Galatians 1:5; 1 Peter 4:11; Revelation 1:18). This means unending time, not an ending to time. In fact, there is no New Testament Greek word for eternity. Further, the Hebrews thought of time on a linear basis, in which history is divided into two stages. The first, this age, is evil; the second, the age to come, is good.

6 Pseudepigrapha are those Jewish writings that were excluded from the Old Testament canon and that find no place in the Apocrypha.

7 Also see Romans 12:2; 1 Corinthians 2:6; Galatians 1:4.

8 George Ladd, *A Theology of the New Testament*, page 48.

9 I do not imply a dualism – Satan equal in power to Christ. Any authority that Satan has is derived from God. For a time, God has permitted Satan to afflict the world so Christ's mercy and judgement can be demonstrated in creation, especially in his work on the cross.

10 The terms 'kingdom of heaven' and 'kingdom of God' are used interchangeably in the New Testament.

11 The Greek word used in New Testament for church, *ekklesia*, was also used in the Greek translation of the Old Testament (the Septuagint). This literally means 'the called out ones', again indicating that the New Testament church stands in direct continuity with the Old Testament people of God.

12 George Ladd, *A Theology of the New Testament*, page 117.

13 Ibid., pg 118.

14 For greater depth in this entire section, see Ladd, *A Theology of the New Testament*, pages 111–19.

15 Jesus came into the world to save men and women from Satan, to forgive and regenerate us, to offer eternal life to all who believe in him. The focus of this book is signs and wonders for the purpose of overcoming Satan's kingdom and as an avenue for leading many to Christ. By focusing on signs and wonders I imply neither that they are the totality of our salvation, nor that the analogy of the church as an army is the only way to understand her. We are also called a family, a refuge, a people, a nation, and so on – each connoting different aspects of God's purpose in salvation.

16 James Kallas, *The Real Satan*, page 60.

17 George Ladd, *The Presence of the Future* (Grand Rapids, Michigan: William B. Eerdmans Publishing Company, 1974), pages 160–6.

18 Ibid., page 162.

Chapter 2

1 There are many questions about demonisation raised in this illustration and throughout the chapter. For example, what is the relationship between personality disorders and demon possession? How can one tell the difference between the two? Questions like these are important but regretfully not the focus of this book. My purpose in raising these questions here is so that the reader understands I am only dealing with one aspect of a complex subject. I refer you to the bibliography for further reading on deliverance.

2 Alan R. Tippett, *People Movements in Southern Polynesia* (Chicago: Moody Press, 1971).

3 C. Peter Wagner, 'Special Kinds of Church Growth', unpublished class notes, Fuller Theological Seminary, 1984, page 14.

4 Alan Tippett, *People Movements*, page 81.

5 Oscar Cullman, *Christ and Time* (London: SCM, 1951) page 64.
6 Karl Ludwig Schmidt, '*Ethnos* in the NT,' *Theological Dictionary of the New Testament*, vol. II (Grand Rapids, Michigan: Eerdmans Publishing Company, 1964), p. 369.
7 See appendices A and B, where I give illustrations of power encounters in the history of the church.
8 Kevin Springer, several months after speaking at Emmaus Fellowship, a church in Ann Arbor, Michigan, in November 1984 received this letter from Martha Slaughter, a woman he prayed for that day:

> I wanted to share with you my experiences since you prayed over me at Emmaus. I had asked you to pray for a spirit of bitterness and resentment to leave. You did that and then stopped and said you felt there was something more – and then said you thought I had a very hard time trusting people. You prayed over me for an anointing of God's own trust for people. I want to share with you that even after church I just *felt* trusting and felt the Lord doing something different in my relationships with the sisters. I felt the Lord ministering the love he has for me through them.
>
> When we came home from church and were discussing everything I shared with Gary [her husband] that I wanted to go and talk with Dr. Dave King (a Christian counsellor). That was significant in itself in that I never would have been open to that at all before. I've been under bondage to mistrust and letting circumstances get the best of me, to the point of sinking into self-pity and letting depression set in. The Lord showed me that he wanted to get these things taken care of once and for all, that he had victory for me and wanted to heal all these areas in me to enable me to go on with him, free of all encumbrances.
>
> Dr. King has been a blessing to both of us and has helped us uncover a lot of garbage. It has been like turning a light on – the searching light of God's Spirit. The Lord has really used the counselling to reveal some bad patterns in relating with people that I had developed just from the way I had been raised and through subsequent relationships before and after I came to the Lord. It has been incredible!
>
> The amazing thing to me is just how gentle and loving and merciful God's 'spiritual surgery' is! The Lord also used two times I was prayed over and literally fell to the floor to do a lot of his work. I have never felt condemned by God as he points out all these problem areas, only tremendously reassured of his love and pleasure in me. I have previously had a problem in feeling condemned by everything.

9 Anonymous, 'Where the Spirit of the Lord Is', in *New Covenant,* October 1978, pages 15–16.
10 Werner Foerster, *'Exousia', Theological Dictionary of the New Testament,* vol II page 568.

Chapter 3

1 I do not mean to imply that power evangelism is the only kind of evangelism practised in the New Testament. Nor do I imply that power evangelism has been the most common type practised by Christians throughout church history. For example, evangelicals assert that the proclamation of the gospel message has intrinsic spiritual power, an assertion I would not deny. But my point remains: power evangelism was one of the normal kinds of evangelism in the early church and has surfaced throughout the history of the church with remarkable results.
2 Sources: The Gallup Poll (1983) and *The Yearbook of American and Canadian Churches* (1967 to 1983).
3 Joseph Bayly, 'Keeping In Step: How Far Will American Evangelicals Follow Secular Cultural Trends?' *Pastoral Renewal*, October 1984, p. 34.
4 See the National Opinion Research Center (NORC – affiliated with the University of Chicago) annual General Social Survey for 1983.
5 C. Peter Wagner, 'A Third Wave?' *Pastoral Renewal*, July–August 1983, pp. 1–5.
6 This statistic, an estimate, comes from many conversations with leading missiologists at Fuller Theological Seminary's School of World Missions. Cf. Craig Hanscome, 'Predicting Missionary Dropout', in the *Evangelical Missions Quarterly*, 1979, pp. 152–5.
7 D. Martyn Lloyd-Jones, *Joy Unspeakable* (Eastbourne: Kingsway Publications, 1984), page 75.
8 C. S. Lewis, *Mere Christianity* (London: Fontana, 1970).

Chapter 4

1 Viggo Sogaard, MA project, 'Commission to Communicate: Cassettes in Context of a Total Christian Communication Program,' Wheaton Graduate School, Wheaton, Illinois, 1973. Also, cf. Viggo Sogaard, *Everything You Need to Know for a Cassette Ministry*, (Minneapolis: Bethany Publishing Company, 1975).
2 James Engel and Wilbert Norton, *What's Gone Wrong with the Harvest?* (Grand Rapids, Michigan: Zondervan Publishing Company, 1975), page 45.

Chapter 5

1 James Sire, *The Universe Next Door* (Leicester; IVP, 1976), page 17.
2 Charles Kraft, *Christianity in Culture*, (Maryknoll: Orbis Books, 1979).
3 Ibid., page 53.
4 Ibid.
5 Harry Blamires, *The Christian Mind*, (London; SPCK, 1963), page 44.
6 Ibid., page 67.
7 Ibid., page 86.
8 Ibid., page 106.
9 Jack Rogers, *Confessions of a Conservative Evangelical*, (Philadelphia: The Westminster Press, 1974), pages 33–34.
10 Paul Hiebert, 'The Flaw of the Excluded Middle', *Missiology:* January, 1982, pages 35–47.
11 Kraft, *Christianity and Culture*, page 60. Dr. Kraft has shown how this assumption/conclusion process works. Here are some cultural features, with a list of assumptions and the conclusions that are reached using each one:

Cultural Feature	Assumption	Conclusion
Clothing	1. Immodest to go naked (USA)	1. Must wear clothes even to bed.
	2. One covers one's body if hiding something (Gava people Nigeria)	2. Go naked to prove yourself.
	3. For ornamentation only (Higi people Nigeria)	3. Wear on 'occasion' only. Rearrange or change in public.
Buying	1. Impersonal, economic transaction (USA)	1. Fixed prices. No interest in seller as person. Get it over quickly.
	2. Social, person-to-person (Africa, Asia, Latin America)	2. Dicker over price. Establish personal relationship. Take time.
Youthfulness	1. Desirable (USA)	1. Look young, act young. Cosmetics.

	2. Tolerated. To be overcome (Africa)	2. Prove yourself mature. Don't act young.
Age	1. Undesirable (USA)	1. Dreaded. Old people unwanted.
	2. Desirable (Africa)	2. Old people revered.
Education	1. Primarily formal, outside home, teacher-centred (USA)	1. Formal schools. Hired specialists.
	2. Primarily informal, in the home, learner-centred, traditional (Africa)	2. Learn by doing. Discipleship. Proverbs and folktales.

Chapter 6

1 Herman Ridderbos, *The Coming of the Kingdom* (Philadelphia: Presbyterian and Reformed, 1962), pages xi–xxxiv.
2 C. Peter Wagner, *Church Growth and the Whole Gospel* (San Francisco: Harper and Row, 1981). Also see Luke 4:18–19; 7:21–22; Mark 16:17–18. (Note that I have added calming storms and feeding thousands.)
3 Ibid.
4 Revelation 21:1; cf. Colin Brown, *The New International Dictionary of New Testament Theology*, vol. 2 (Exeter: Paternoster, 1976), page 631.
5 *Evangelicals and Social Concern, an Evangelical Commitment*, No. 21, Grand Rapids Report, 1982, pages 9–11, 30–32.
6 James Dunn, *Jesus and the Spirit* (London: SCM, 1975), pages 48–9.
7 Edward Langton, *Essentials of Demonology: A Study of Jewish and Christian Doctrine, Its Origin and Development* (London, 1949), page 173.
8 Jairus's daughter: Matthew 9:18–26; Mark 5:21–43; Luke 8:40–56. Lazarus: John 11:1–12:19. The widow's son: Luke 7:11–17; 'holy people' at the crucifixion: Matthew 27:52.

Chapter 7

1 Robert K. Johnston, editor. *The Use of the Bible in Theology – Evangelical Options* (Atlanta, Georgia: John Knox, 1985).

2 Signs and wonders –
Example

Result

By disciples – Acts 2:43

Daily adding to church – 2:47

Power of God shown in mighty works – 4:33

Philip – 8:6

Samaria Church – 8:12

Hand of Lord with them 11:20–21 and 13:11

Great number believed and turned to the Lord – 11:21

Full of Spirit – 11:24

Lord added to the church – 11:24

Paul and Barnabas – 14:1–7

Believers – 14:4

Extraordinary miracles/ teaching at Ephesus – 19:11

All churches in book of Revelation started during these two years

3 Speaking gifts –
Example

Result

Tongues – Acts 10:44

Baptised believers – 10:47

Prophecy – 13:1

Conversion of John the Baptist's disciples – 19:5–7

Tongues/prophecy – 19:1–7

4 Visions –
Example

Result

Paul, Macedonian – Acts 16:8

European churches

Paul – 18:9

Church at Corinth

5 Miracles –
Example

Result

Ananias/Sapphira – 5:1–11

Fear – 5:13

Spirit caught up Philip – 8:39

Paul blinded – 9:1–9a

Elymas blinded – 13:4–12

Sergius Paulus believed

Paul stoned/raised – 14:19–20

Disciples – 14:21

6 Healings –
Example

Result

Lame man – 3:7,8

Added to 5,000 – 4:4

Sick and unclean spirits – 5:16

Healed – 5:16

Paul's blindness healed – 9:17–19

Lame man – Lystra – 14:10

Disciples – 14:21

Demon expelled – 16:18

Brethren – 16:40

| Publius's father – fever/ dysentery – 28:8 | | All sick on island healed – 28:9 Church started according to church historians |

7 Angelic visitation –

Example		*Result*
Peter – 12:7		
Paul – 27:23,24		

8

Signs and Wonders	*Preaching*	*Church Growth*
2:4	2:14	2:41
3:1	3:12	4:4
8:6	8:6	8:12
8:26	8:35	8:38
10:3,12,44	10:34	10:47
11:20–21	11:20	11:21
11:23,24	11:23	11:24b
13:1–3		Churches in Asia, Europe
14:1–7	14:3	14:4,21,22
14:8–18	14:15	14:21
16:16	16:14	16:40
16:25,26	16:31	16:34
18:1	18:5	18:8
19:11	19:10	Churches in Asia

9 J. Sidlow Baxter, *Divine Healing of the Body* (Grand Rapids: Zondervan Publishing House, 1979), page 52.

Chapter 8

1 C. Peter Wagner, 'A Third Wave?' *Pastoral Renewal*, July–August 1983, pages 1–5.
2 Ibid., page 4.
3 Richard Ostling in 'Counting Every Soul on Earth', *Time*, 3 May, 1982, pages 66–67.
4 Constance Jacquet, *Yearbook of American and Canadian Churches*, (Nashville, 1983), page 225.
5 Ibid., page 226.
6 Elmer Towns, 'The World's Ten Largest Churches', *Christian Life*, January 1983, pages 60–66.
7 Victor Monterosso, William Reed, and Harman Johnson, *Latin American Church Growth*, (Grand Rapids, William B. Eerdmans, 1969) page 58.

8 Peter Wagner, *What Are We Missing?* (Carol Stream, Illinois: Creation House, 1973), page 25.

9 C. Peter Wagner, *Your Spiritual Gifts* (Glendale, California: Regal, 1979), page 32.

10 Vinson Synan, *In the Latter Days*, (Ann Arbor, Michigan, Servant Books, 1984), page 74.

11 Ibid., pages 74–5.

12 Synan, *The Holiness-Pentecostal Movement in the United States*, (Grand Rapids, Michigan, William B. Eerdmans, 1972), page 144.

13 Synan, *In the Latter Days*, page 79.

14 Ibid., page 80.

15 Ibid., page 81.

16 David Barrett, *World Christian Encyclopedia* (Oxford, 1982), pages 1–104.

17 Richard Quebedeaux, *The Young Evangelicals*, (London: Harper & Row, 1974), page 42.

18 Dean Hoge, *Converts, Dropouts, and Returnees* (Washington, D.C.: United States Catholic Conference, 1981).

19 Michael Cassidy, *Bursting the Wineskins*, (London: Hodder and Stoughton, 1983), page 19. Also, cf. James Davison Hunter, *American Evangelicalism*, (New Brunswick, New Jersey: Rutgers University Press, 1983), page 7.

20 Ibid., page 9; also see Quebedeaux, *The Young Evangelicals*, pages 13, 28–41.

21 John MacArthur, *The Charismatics*, (Grand Rapids, Michigan: Zondervan Publishing Company, 1978), page 131.

22 F. F. Bruce, *1 & 2 Corinthians*, (London: Marshall, Morgan and Scott, 1971) page 122.

23 Hunter, *American Evangelicalism*, pages 41–48.

24 Wagner, 'A Third Wave?', pages 4–5.

Chapter 9

1 Andrew Murray, *The Believer's Full Blessing of Pentecost*, (Basingstoke: Lakeland, 1984), pages 9, 10.

2 A. W. Tozer, *How to Be Filled with the Holy Spirit*, (Harrisburg, Pennsylvania: Christian Publications, Inc.).

3 'A gradual work of grace,' Wesley wrote, 'constantly precedes the instantaneous work both of justification and sanctification, but the work itself is undoubtedly instantaneous . . . after a gradually increasing conviction of inbred sin you will be sanctified in a moment.' (Letter of the 21st of June, 1784, in *The Letters of Rev.*

John Wesley, ed. John Telford. London: The Epworth Press, 1931, pages 221–22.)

4 Vinson Synon, *In the Latter Days*, (Ann Arbor, Michigan: Servant Books, 1984), pages 36–7. Cf. Frederick Dale Bruner, *A Theology of the Holy Spirit*, (London: Hodder and Stoughton, 1970), pages 37–9, 46–7.

5 D. Martyn Lloyd-Jones, *Joy Unspeakable*, (Eastbourne; Kingsway, 1984, p. 80.)

6 Reuben A. Torrey, *The Person and Work of the Holy Spirit*, (New York: Fleming H. Revell Company, 1910), pages 176–210.

7 Torrey, *Baptism in the Holy Ghost* (London: James Nisbet & Company Ltd, 1895), page 16.

8 Synon, *Latter Days*, page 45.

9 See Edward O'Connor, 'Hidden Roots of the Charismatic Renewal in the Catholic Church', in Synan, *Aspects of Pentecostal-Charismatic Origins* (Plainfield, New Jersey: Logos International, 1975), pages 169–92.

10 Russell P. Spittler, 'The Pentecostal Tradition: Reflections of an "Ichthus"-iast', page 5. (An unpublished paper read at the annual meeting of the Evangelical Theological Society, December 27–29, 1971, Gordon-Conwell Theological Seminary, South Hamilton, Mass.)

11 The practice of baptising new converts was (probably) introduced to the Jews by the Hillelites in the late intertestamental period. The Hillelites based the practice on Numbers 15:14 and Exodus 24:8. Cf. Oscar Cullmann, *Baptism in the New Testament* (London: SCM, 1950), pages 11, 25.

12 Charles E. Hummell, *Fire in the Fireplace: Contemporary Charismatic Renewal* (Oxford: Mowbray, 1978), page 185.

13 Russell Spittler, ed. *Perspectives on the New Pentecostalism* (Grand Rapids: Baker Book House, 1976), page 186.

14 Spittler, 'The Pentecostal Tradition', page 5.

15 Ibid.

16 I will not discuss here the theories about the cessation of gifts like tongues. See my comments in chapters 7 and 8.

17 Spittler, 'The Pentecostal Tradition', page 4.

18 Ibid., page 6.

19 C. S. Lewis, *Mere Christianity* (London: Fontana, 1970).

Appendix B

1 Christiaan DeWet, 'Signs and Wonders in Church Growth', a

Masters thesis for Fuller Seminary's School of World Missions, December 1981, pages 93–123.
2 Ibid., pages 95–6, footnote number 3, page 98.
3 Ibid., pages 96–7.
4 Donald O. Young, in 'Signs, Wonders and Church Growth in the Ivory Coast', an unpublished paper written for MC:510 – Signs, Wonders and Church Growth, Fuller Theological Seminary, 1982.
5 Donald McGavran, 'Healing and Evangelisation of the World', Basilia Church Growth Seminar, 1979, syllabus, page 296.
6 DeWet, pages 102, 106; cf 'But What About Hicks?' *Christian Century*, July 7, 1954, pp 814–815.
7 McGavran, 'Divine Healing and Church Growth', an address delivered before a gathering of Christian and Missionary Alliance missionaries in Lincoln, Nebraska, 1979.
8 R. R. Cunville, 'The Evangelisation of Northeast India', an unpublished D.Miss. thesis for Fuller Seminary's School of World Missions, 1975, pages 156–79.
9 G. Elford, 'Signs and Wonders Among the Canadian Indians', an unpublished paper written for MC:510 at Fuller Seminary.

BIBLIOGRAPHY

The Apostolic Fathers. London: Thomas Nelson.
   Vol. 3. *Barnabas and the Didache.* 1965. Robert Kraft, ed.
   Vol. 4. *Ignatius of Antioch.* 1966. Robert Grant, ed.
   Vol. 6. *Hermas.* Graydon F. Snyder, ed.
Baird, Henry. 1895. *The Huguenots.* New York: Charles Scribner. Vols. 1–2.
Baring-Gould, S. 1897. *The Lives of the Saints.* London: John Nimmo. Vol. 3.
Barker, Glenn; William Lane and J. Ramsey Michaels. 1969. *The New Testament Speaks.* New York: Harper & Row.
Barrett, David. 1982. *World Christian Encyclopedia.* Oxford: Oxford University Press.
Barrett, Thomas Ball. 1927. *When the Fire Fell.* Oslo, Norway: Hansen and Soner.
Bartleman, Frank. 1980. *Azusa Street.* Plainfield: Logos.
Baxter, J. Sidlow. 1979. *Divine Healing of the Body.* Grand Rapids, Michigan: Zondervan Publishing House.
Bennett, Dennis. 1970. *Nine O'Clock in the Morning.* Eastbourne: Coverdale House.
Blamires, Harry. 1978. *The Christian Mind.* London: SPCK.
idem. 1980. *Where Do We Stand?* Ann Arbor, Michigan: Servant Publications.
Bosworth, F. F. 1973. *Christ the Healer.* Old Tappan, New Jersey: Fleming H. Revell.
Bresson, Bernard L. 1966. *Studies in Ecstasy.* New York: Vantage Press.
Brown, Colin. ed. 1976. *The New International Dictionary of New Testament Theology.* Exeter: The Paternoster Press. 3 vols.
Bruce, F. F. 1971. *1 and 2 Corinthians.* London: Marshall, Morgan and Scott.
Brumback, Carl. 1961. *Suddenly From People.* Springfield, Missouri: Gospel Publishing House.

Bruner, Frederick Dale. 1970. *A Theory of the Holy Spirit, The Pentecostal Experience and the New Testament*. London: Hodder and Stoughton.

Cassidy, Michael. 1983. *Bursting the Wineskins*. London: Hodder and Stoughton.

The Catholic Encyclopedia Dictionary. 1941. New York: The Gilmary Society.

Christenson, Larry. 1972. *A Message to the Charismatic Movement*. Weymouth, Massachusetts: Dimension.

Cho, Paul Yonggi. 1979. *The Fourth Dimension*. Plainfield: Logos International.

Coxe, A. Cleveland. 1951. *The Ante-Nicene Fathers*. Grand Rapids, Michigan: Eerdmans Publishing Company, Vol. 1, 3, 4, 5, 6.

Cross, Whitney R. 1950. *The Burned-over District*. New York: Harper & Row.

Cullmann, Oscar. 1951. *Christ and Time*. London: SCM.

idem. 1950. *Baptism in the New Testament*. London: SCM.

Curnock, Nehemiah. ed. nd. *The Journal of John Wesley*. London: Charles Kelley. Vol. 1, 2, 3.

Defferari, Joseph. nd. *The Fathers of the Church*. Washington, D.C.: The Catholic University of America Press.

Vol. 9. St. Basil, *Ancetial Works*.

Vol. 15. *Early Christian Biographies*.

Vol. 24. St. Augustine. *City of God*. Books 17–22.

Vol. 25. St. Hilary of Poitiers. *The Trinity*.

Vol. 39. St. Gregory the Great. *Dialogues*.

Vol. 44. St. Ambrose. *Theological and Dogmatic Works*.

Vol. 58. St. Gregory of Nyssa. *Ascetical Works*.

Dix, Gregory. ed. 1968. *The Treatise of the Apostolic Tradition*. London: SPCK.

Douglas, J. D. ed. 1974. *The New International Dictionary of the Christian Church*. Exeter: Paternoster Press.

Drummond, Andrew L. nd. *Edward Irving and His Circle*. London: James Clark & Co.

Dunn, James D. G. 1970. *Baptism in the Holy Spirit*. London: SCM.

idem. 1975. *Jesus and The Spirit*. London: SCM.

Dudden, F. Homes. 1905. *Gregory the Great*. New York: Russell & Russell.

Easton, Burton. ed. 1934. *The Apostolic Tradition of Hippolytos*. Cambridge: Cambridge University Press.

Elliot, Elisabeth. 1981. *The Savage My Kinsman*. Ann Arbor, Michigan: Servant Books.

Elford. 1983. *Signs and Wonders Among the Canadian Indians*. Unpublished.

Engel, James and Wilbert, Norton. 1975. *What's Gone Wrong with the Harvest?* Grand Rapids, Zondervan.

Fordsham, Stanley, 1948. Smith Wigglesworth: *Apostle of Faith*. Springfield: Radiant Books.

Fox, George. 1901. *The Journal of George Fox*. London: Friends Tract Association. 2 Vol.

Frazier, Claude. ed. 1973. *Faith Healing: Finger of God? or Scientific Curiosity?* New York: Thomas Nelson.

Gibbs, Eddie. 1981. *I Believe in Church Growth*. London: Hodder & Stoughton.

Giles, John A. ed. nd. *The Venerable Bede's Ecclesiastical History of England*. London.

Gordon, A. J. 1802. *The Ministry of Healing*. Harrisburg: Christian Publication Inc.

Grant, Robert M. 1971. *Augustine to Constantine*. London: Collins.

idem. 1946. *Second Century Christianity*. London: SPCK.

Green, Michael, 1975. *I Believe in the Holy Spirit.* London: Hodder & Stoughton.

Grossman, Siegfried. 1971. *Charisma: The Gifts of the Spirit*. Wheaton: Key Publications.

Harper, Michael. 1965. *As at the Beginning: The Twentieth Century Pentecostal Revival*. London: Hodder & Stoughton.

idem. 1979. *Three Sisters*. Wheaton, Illinois: Tyndale House Publishers.

Harrell, David Allen, 1975. *All Things Are Possible*. Bloomington: Indiana University Press.

Hermann, Placid. ed. nd. *St. Francis of Assisi*. Chicago: Herald Press.

Hoge, Dean. 1981. *Converts, Dropouts, and Returnees*. Washington, D.C.: United States Catholic Conference.

Hummel, Charles E. 1978. *Fire in the Fireplace*. Oxford: Mowbrays.

Hunter, A. M. 1980. *Christ and the Kingdom*. Edinburgh: The Saint Andrew Press.

Hunter, James Davison, 1983. *American Evangelicalism*. New Brunswick, New Jersey: Rutgers University Press.

Jacquet, Constance. 1983. *Yearbook of American and Canadian Churches*. Nashville.

Johnston, Robert K., editor. 1985. *The Use of the Bible in Theology – Evangelical Options*. Atlanta, Georgia: John Knox.

Kallas, James. 1966. *The Satanward View; A Study in Pauline Theology*. Philadelphia: The Westminster Press.

idem. 1968. *Jesus and The Power of Satan*. Philadelphia: The Westminster Press.

idem. 1975. *The Real Satan*. Minneapolis: Augsburg Publishing House.

Kavanaugh, Kienan. ed. 1976. *The Collected Works of St. Teresa of Avila*. Washington D.C.: ICS Publications.

Kelsey, Morton T. 1964. *Tongue Speaking: An Experiment in Spiritual Experience*. New York: Doubleday & Company.

idem. 1968. *Tongues Speaking*. London: Hodder and Stoughton.

idem. 1973. *Healing and Christianity*. London: SCM.

Kittel, G. ed. 1964. *Theological Dictionary of the New Testament*. Grand Rapids, Eerdmans.

Kraft, Charles H. 1979. *Christianity in Culture*. Maryknoll: Orbis Books.

Kreiser, Robert. 1978. *Miracles, Convulsions, and Ecclesiastical Politics in Early Eighteenth-Century Paris*. Princeton: Princeton University Press.

Ladd, George Eldon. 1964. *Jesus and the Kingdom*. London: Harper & Row.

idem. 1974. *A Theology of the New Testament*. Guildford: Lutterworth Press.

idem. 1974. *The Presence of the Future*. Grand Rapids, Eerdmans.

Langton, Edward. 1949. *Essentials of Demonology: A Study of Jewish and Christian Doctrine, Its Origin and Development*. London.

Lasch, Christopher. 1977. *Haven in a Heartless World*. New York: Basic Books, Inc.

Laurentin, Rene. 1978. *Catholic Pentecostalism*. London: Darton, Longman and Todd.

Lindsell, Harold. 1983. *The Holy Spirit in the Latter Days*. Nashville, Thomas Nelson.

Lloyd-Jones, D. Martyn. 1984. *Joy Unspeakable*. Eastbourne: Kingsway Publications.

Martin, Ralph. 1975. *Fire on the Earth*. Ann Arbor, Michigan: Servant Books.

MacArthur, John. 1978. *The Charismatics*. Grand Rapids: Zondervan Publishing Company.

MacNutt, Francis. 1974. *Healing*. Tenbury Wells: Fowler Wright Books Ltd.

McDonald, William. G. gen. ed. 1967. *New Catholic Encyclopedia*. Washington D.C.: The Catholic University of America. Vol. 14.

McDonnell, Kilian, and Arnold Bittlinger. 1972. *The Baptism of the Holy Spirit as an Ecumenical Problem*. South Bend, Indiana: Charismatic Renewal Services.

Monden, Louis. 1960. *Signs and Wonders*. New York: Desclee.

Monterosso, Victor, William Reed, and Harman Johnson. 1969. *Latin American Church Growth*. Grand Rapids: Eerdmans.

Moore, Louis. nd. *The Visitor*. np.

Murray, Andrew. 1984. *The Believer's Full Blessing of Pentecost.* Basingstoke: Lakeland.

Nickalls, John. ed. 1975. *The Journal of George Fox.* London: Religious Society of Friends.

Olsson, Karl A. 1962. *By One Spirit.* Chicago: Covenant Press.

Oswald, Hilton. ed. nd. *Luther's Works.* Saint Louis: Concordia Publishing House. Vol. 25.

Packer, James I. 1984. *Keep in Step with the Spirit.* Leicester: IVP.

Penn-Lewis, Jessie. nd. *The Awakening in Wales.* Ft. Washington: Christian Literature Crusade.

Pilkington, J. G. ed. 1963. *The Confessions of St. Augustine.* New York: Liveright Publishing Co.

Price, Charles S. 1972. *And Signs Followed.* Plainfield: Logos.

Quebedeaux, Richard. 1974. *The Young Evangelicals.* London: Harper & Row.

idem. 1976. *The New Charismatics.* New York: Doubleday.

idem. 1978. *The Worldly Evangelicals.* New York: Harper & Row.

idem. 1983. *The New Charismatics II: How a Christian Renewal Movement Became Part of the American Religious Mainstream.* San Francisco: Harper & Row.

Rahner, Karl. 1962. *Spiritual Exercises.* London: Herder and Herder.

Ranaghan, Kevin, and Dorothy Ranaghan. 1969. *Catholic Pentecostals.* Paramus, New Jersey: Paulist Press.

Rogers, Jack. 1974. *Confessions of a Conservative Evangelical.* Philadelphia: The Westminster Press.

Ridderbos, Herman. 1962. *The Coming of the Kingdom.* Philadelphia: Presbyterian and Reformed.

Sandford, John and Paula Sandford. 1982. *The Transformation of the Inner Man.* South Plainfield, New Jersey: Bridge Publishing, Inc.

Schaff, Philip and Henry Wace. nd. *Nicene and Post-Nicene Fathers.* Grand Rapids: Eerdmans Publishing Company. Series 1: Vol. 1, 7, 8, 12, 16. Series 2: Vol. 1, 6, 7.

Sire, James. 1977. *The Universe Next Door.* Leicester: IVP.

idem. 1980. *Scripture Twisting.* Downers Grove: InterVarsity Press.

Sogaard, Viggo. 1984. Unpublished Ph.D. dissertation, Fuller Theological Seminary, Pasadena, California.

Spittler, Russell P. 1971. 'The Pentecostal Tradition: Reflections of an "Ichthus"-iast" unpublished paper.

idem. ed. 1976. *Perspectives on the New Pentecostalism.* Grand Rapids: Baker Book House.

Synan, Vinson. 1972. *The Holiness-Pentecostal Movement in the United States.* Grand Rapids, Michigan: William B. Eerdmans.

idem. 1974. *Charismatic Bridges.* Ann Arbor, Michigan: Word of Life.

idem. 1984. *In the Latter Days.* Ann Arbor, Michigan: Servant Books.

Tappert, Theodore B. ed. nd. *Luther: Letters of Spiritual Counsel.* The Library of Christian Classics. Philadelphia: The Westminster Press. Vol. 18.

Telford, John. ed. 1931. *The Letters of John Wesley.* London: Epworth. Vol. 2.

Thompson, A. H. ed. nd. *Bede, His Life, Times and Writings.* London: Oxford Press.

Tippett, Alan R. 1971. *People Movements in Southern Polynesia.* Chicago: Moody Press.

Tozer, A. W. *How to Be Filled with the Holy Spirit.* Harrisburg, Pennsylvania: Christian Publications, Inc.

Torrey, Reuben A. 1910. *The Person and Work of the Holy Spirit.* New York: Fleming H. Revell Company.

idem. 1895. *Baptism in the Holy Ghost.* London: James Nisbet & Company Ltd.

Tydings, Judith. nd. *Gathering A People.* np.

Vine, W. E. 1940. *An Expository Dictionary of New Testament Words.* Basingstoke: Oliphants.

Vos, Geerhardus. 1972. *The Kingdom of God and the Church.* Nutley, New Jersey: Presbyterian and Reformed Publishing Company.

Wagner, C. Peter. 1972. *Frontiers in Missionary Strategy.* Chicago: Moody Press.

idem. 1973. *What Are We Missing?* (Formerly titled *Look Out! the Pentecostals Are Coming*) Carol Stream, Illinois: Creation House.

idem. 1976a. *Your Church Can Grow.* Ventura, California: Regal Books.

idem. 1976b. *Your Spiritual Gifts Can Help Your Church Grow.* Ventura, California: Regal Books.

idem. 1981. *Church Growth and Whole Gospel.* New York: Harper and Row.

idem. 1983. *On the Crest of the Wave.* Ventura, California: Regal Books.

Warfield, Benjamin B. 1918. *Counterfeit Miracles.* Edinburgh: The Banner of Truth Trust.

Warren, Max. 1976. *I Believe in the Great Commission.* London: Hodder & Stoughton.

Watson, David. 1976. *I Believe in Evangelism.* London: Hodder & Stoughton.

idem. 1981. *Called & Committed.* London: Hodder & Stoughton.

Wells, David. 1972. *Revolution in Rome.* London: Tyndale.

Woodworth-Etter, Maria. 1976. *Her Life and Ministry.* Dallas: Christ for the Nation.